Epiphany

ARMOUR

innovo
PUBLISHING

Published by
Innovo Publishing, LLC
www.innovopublishing.com
1-888-546-2111

Providing Full-Service Publishing Services for Christian Authors, Artists &
Ministries: Books, eBooks, Audiobooks, Music, Film & Courses

EPIPHANY

ISBN: 978-1-61314-555-5

Cover Design & Interior Layout: Innovo Publishing, LLC

Printed in the United States of America
U.S. Printing History
First Edition: 2019

CONTENTS

INTRODUCTION

Epiphany has been celebrated by Christians from the earliest days of the Church. Although no date of establishment can be validated through historical texts with certainty, the day has been observed for almost as long as have Christmas and Easter. Unlike Christmas and Easter, though, Epiphany was to fade or be jettisoned by significant segments of Christendom and ultimately ignored by or unknown to the majority of believers.

Epiphany was set from the beginning on January 6th. From reading the texts of Matthew 2 and Luke 2, church leaders realized that the Magi had not actually been present on the night of Jesus' birth. Though the precise amount of time that elapsed between His birth and the arrival of the Magi in Bethlehem cannot be known, the two weeks symbolically allotted by the Church fathers would seem a reasonable guess, but any speculation ranging from a month to a year later also lay within the realm of possibility.

The reason for the establishment of Epiphany as a holy day was the belief on the part of many who had studied the Scripture that the Magi had experienced an epiphany upon seeing Jesus at the end of their journey. As they brought forth their gifts and looked into the child's eyes, they suddenly recognized the King of Kings, Lord of Lords, and the Savior for all people. Thus they realized long before most others the spiritual and universal nature of the Kingdom to be established by this child.

The word "epiphany" as defined in the dictionary reads in part as follows:

> ...an appearance or manifestation esp.
> of a divine being. ...(1): a usually sudden

manifestation or perception of the essential nature or meaning of something. (2) an intuitive grasp of reality through something (as an event) usually simple and striking (3) an illuminating discovery, realization, or disclosure b: a revealing scene or moment.

In simple terms, an epiphany is something realized, made known, or revealed.

That the Magi experienced an epiphany with regard to the identity and role of Jesus and the nature of His kingdom is indisputable. As to when that epiphany occurred, there can be reasonable debate. What we are given in the text would seem to suggest that the epiphany actually came to the Magi much earlier, even before they commenced their long journey.

Another reason for the establishment of the holy day of Epiphany likely lay in the fact that the majority of Christians were Gentiles residing somewhere other than the Holy Land. In the arrival, worship, gifts, and departure for home of Persian Magi, many saw what they considered to be a foreshadowing of Jesus' mission, as prophesied by Simeon in Luke 2:32, to be "A Light of Revelation To The Gentiles." Though the Gospel of Christ was obviously yet to be given, we might even suggest that, at some level and with some capacity of understanding, the gospel, or a proto-gospel, went out from Israel for the first time with the return of the Magi to the East. What they had seen and the epiphany experienced doubtless would not be kept to themselves. That what they had been given to understand was something wholly different and unprecedented in the affairs of men and religion would not have been lost on them.

A final factor that likely played a role in prompting the establishment of Epiphany was the Church fathers' realization that many professing Christians were still celebrating Christmas in the same way that the Romans long had celebrated the winter solstice with substantial drinking and partying and little acknowledgement of any spiritual element. Such a pattern of celebration had proven difficult to alter. To follow Christmas with a two-week period culminating in a holy day that would be statedly and solely spiritual seemed a way to return the focus of believers back to the true essence of, and reason for, the solemn remembrance of the birth of Christ.

Initially, the concept was successful. Many, in the two weeks leading up to January 6th, returned to or maintained a spiritual focus. They pondered and celebrated the brotherhood of all believers in Christ regardless of race, nation, or tongue in the spiritual kingdom with neither frontiers nor borders as symbolized by the Magi returning home with their epiphany.

Augustine of Hippo, one of the foremost of the early Church Fathers, was surely a powerful preacher and an astute theologian. His understanding of history, however, left something to be desired. Unwittingly, he set into motion significant and, perhaps, largely irreparable damage to the observance of Epiphany. Greatly, ridiculously and needlessly embellishing the account in Matthew 2, Augustine turned the Magi into kings. Tertullian, at an earlier time, also had errantly referred to them as kings.

The result was that monarchs and royal families the world over took the two Church Fathers' errant ramblings as a divine carte blanche to celebrate themselves and to mandate that all within their respective domains pay homage to their rule through days of drunken festivities. While a few of the most devout kept the spiritual observance of Epiphany, the bulk of the masses ceased to contemplate the significance of the arrival and departure of the Magi and of the gifts that they presented to the newborn King of Kings. The levels of drinking and raucous partying soon rose to rival that of any Roman Winter Solstice celebration, and even the name of the holy day itself largely disappeared. Epiphany became known as King's Day, a designation that remains to this day in parts of Latin America and Europe.

Midway through the 19th century, however, significant changes in the celebration of the holiday season became evident. Due to efforts of devoted clergymen and support from the British royal family, the spiritual remembrances of Christmas began to be embraced anew by gathered families both in northern Europe and across the Atlantic in America. The rekindling of the spiritual fire of Christmas seems to have triggered a renewed interest in Epiphany as well, as the holy day of Epiphany came to be considered the final day of the holiday season, which, at that time, began on Christmas Eve.

Epiphany then was the day when all gathered around the Christmas tree one last time to visit, pray, and sing Christmas carols before taking down the ornaments and decorations. Too, in Europe, Latin America, and in much of America, Epiphany was the day upon which gifts were given—a practice still common in parts of Europe and Latin America. Given Epiphany's emphasis upon the significance of the coming of the Magi and the gifts they brought, the custom follows a sound logic. Though customs varied from place to place, children might leave out some grain for the Magi's camels on Epiphany Eve and then awake the next morning to find that the "Magi" had left them a few coins or some other simple gift.

Many at this time also began to mark Epiphany with religious observances of prayer and worship—in churches and in homes—just as had been intended by Church Fathers from the beginning. Around the turn of the 20th century, though, things began to change once more. With the invention and popularization of Santa Claus in America and Father Christmas in Europe—not to mention the massive and ever-expanding marketing campaigns eventually set into motion behind both—virtually all gift giving was shifted to December 25th, which became the focal point for the entire season. With the new trend, increasing secularization and inherent gradual spiritual decline in the hearts and minds of individuals, observances of Epiphany began to fade. While in parts of Europe and Latin America the holy day, whether remembered as Epiphany or King's Day, was never lost and is observed in some form to this day, Epiphany in America faded to the extent that most Americans now know nothing of the day's origins or meaning.

Among the relatively few devout, there have always been those who held to the annual observance of Epiphany. Too, some churches have been consistent over the years in their observances. Perhaps due to some combination of increasing secularization, the growing collective spiritual void, rampant materialism, and the incessant annual attacks upon all Christian symbols and expressions of Christmas, there seems to have been a small resurgence of interest in the observance of Epiphany just as there has been for some time now in the observance of Advent. The practices of keeping Advent and Epiphany, of course, are different. Advent is observed over a period of four weeks, often employs candles and wreaths, and generally follows a selected succession of Scripture or devotional readings. Epiphany is traditionally observed on a single day. The purpose in observing either, however, is very much the same. We focus upon the spiritual essence of what it is that we are to remember and celebrate as we close out the old year and prepare to begin a new one.

In watching the dark of night draw its veil over many Christmas days in years past, I have heard a variety of emotions and thoughts expressed. Some have said that they are just glad when it is all over. With the pressure they feel or put on themselves, the hustle and bustle of the season, the shopping and the presents, reunion of family, the requisite meals and parties, and the travel or other obligations, they are simply relieved to have it all behind them for another year. Many, on the other hand, have expressed feeling down or, perhaps, mild levels of sadness as the eagerly anticipated season of joy comes to an end. The house that had been full of cherished family and friends empties out. All the parties and much-loved traditional foods and meals are finished. Their favorite Christmas movies and music have to be put away for another year, and as the tree, lights, ornaments, and decorations come down, the festivity and warmth seems to have been taken out of the house.

In our home there are no such feelings or thoughts. For as the hour grows late on Christmas night, it is still but the first day of Christmas. Eleven more days of joy, celebration, thought, and reflection lay ahead. Our tree, lights, decorations, and candles all remain as they are through the day of Epiphany. The devotions and meditations of the season of Advent simply shift seamlessly into the devotions, readings, meditations, and prayers of Epiphany. Throughout the twelve days of Christmas, our readings, contemplations, and discussions focus upon Scriptures and the writings coming from our fathers and mothers in the faith with a focus on the implications of the journey and epiphany of the Magi specifically and on the blessed brotherhood of all believers generally. Jesus is the glory of Israel, yet a light unto the Gentiles, who would establish a kingdom eternal of all nations and peoples. Then, on the night of Epiphany in the light of the tree and candles with our favorite Christmas sacred music softly playing, my wife and I share together a Persian dinner with any guests in our home as we contemplate the journey of the Magi back to their home in the East and the invisible gift they carried. The gift not only for them but that which was to be for all peoples of every nation, tribe, and tongue. Finally, as the evening draws to a close, we exchange gifts and cards. Sometimes there are nice gifts, but usually the gifts are quite simple. With them, though, we are reminded of the pleasure and blessings of giving and, most important, remember the ultimate gift offered to all people.

For us, the twelve days of Christmas leading up to Epiphany are, in some respects, the most blessed and enjoyable part of the holiday season. As with many people, the current holiday season, running from Thanksgiving through Christmas Day, tends to be busy for us. The standard festivities of the season and obligations with family, church, friends, and work colleagues have a way of filling up the December calendar quickly. Yet in the days following December 25th, there tends to be a lull. People are worn out. Things slow and quieten down. Obligations are less or none at all for a time. Through these slower, quieter days, we find that we have more time for each other, more time for our favorite Christmas movies and music, and more time to give to reading, study, contemplation, meditation, and prayer. Too, we have opportunity to fellowship with those whom we may have missed through the bustle of the first part of the season. Then time to reflect in full upon the advent of Jesus Christ in Bethlehem and the going out of His light from there through the desert, into the Fertile Crescent, over the Zagros Mountains and into Persia and then unto all the world.

With these thoughts and in this spirit we offer the pages that follow. Consider that on the night of December 25th Christmas does not end but only begins. Embrace the lull and the slowing down in the days that follow to make time for those you may have missed or overlooked in previous days. In thought, readings, prayer, and meditation, delve more deeply into the spiritual truths that are the essence of what we are to remember and celebrate. Examine your own life and actions in the year that is coming to an end, and then consider what can be done better in the new year to come. Reflect upon the magnitude and beauty of the gift from the living God of His

Son as the light, ransom, and atonement for the salvation of all people. Contemplate the gold, frankincense, and myrrh; but, more important, consider what will be your own "gold, frankincense, and myrrh"—the gifts you will bring to others in Jesus' love and name. As the Magi sought and travelled far, consider what it truly means and entails to seek Him with all your mind and heart. Finally, because the Gospel Light did go out from Israel, appreciate the brotherhood in Christ you share with so many of every race, culture, tongue, and nation in His Kingdom without borders, boundaries, or end.

PROLOGUE

¹ Listen to Me, O islands,
And pay attention, you peoples from afar.
The Lord called Me from the womb;
From the body of My mother He named Me.
² He has made My mouth like a sharp sword,
In the shadow of His hand He has concealed Me;
And He has also made Me a select arrow,
He has hidden Me in His quiver.
³ He said to Me, "You are My Servant, Israel,
In Whom I will show My glory."
⁴ But I said, "I have toiled in vain,
I have spent My strength for nothing and vanity;
Yet surely the justice due to Me is with the Lord,
And My reward with My God."
⁵ And now says the Lord, who formed Me from the womb to be His Servant,
To bring Jacob back to Him, so that Israel might be gathered to Him
(For I am honored in the sight of the Lord,
And My God is My strength),
⁶ He says, "It is too small a thing that You should be My Servant
To raise up the tribes of Jacob and to restore the preserved ones of Israel;
I will also make You a light of the nations
So that My salvation may reach to the end of the earth."

Isaiah 49:1-6

To many who believed as well as to unbelievers, the way and message of Jesus Christ came as a surprise. Few Gentiles knew anything about a Messiah who would come to establish a kingdom on earth; but to most Jews, the coming Messiah was the one who not only would redeem Israel but would also reestablish her sovereignty and military power as well as make her enemies her footstool forevermore.

In retrospect it becomes clear that the message and way of the Messiah, our Lord Jesus Christ, should not have seemed so strange or surprising. For through the long years of darkness, disobedience, and the degeneration of the sacred covenant, the prophets had spoken, and regarding the mission of the coming Messiah, they had spoken lucidly.

Now He waited, a select arrow concealed in the quiver of His Father, but in His Father's time He would be drawn, nocked, and let fly. He would come down to us as one of us and the words of His mouth would go forth like a sharp sword, piercing all men as far as the division of soul and spirit and revealing the true thoughts and intentions of every heart. The glory and salvation of His chosen people Israel He would be, but there was more. He would be a light for all the nations, so that His salvation and truth would reach to the ends of the earth. He would take the throne of David forevermore, and His kingdom would have neither borders nor end. People from every nation would call upon Him in every tongue. In the islands of the Pacific, Atlantic, and Indian Oceans, to the far eastern reaches of Asia, south to the darkest, forbidding depths of Africa, north up through the most isolated regions of Europe, west to a New World resting between the two great oceans, then further south still unto the austral realm.

This the prophets had foreseen, and of this they had prophesied. Yet echoes and memories of the prophets' words had faded amid an ever-deepening spiritual darkness. Among a few faithful there remained a faint but flickering light of anticipation fueled by the yearning and hope of persevering faith—a light made manifest only in the depths of their own hearts.

The veil of nighttime over Judah was full and dark, but in the still silence of night a strange star appeared. Men far away to the east saw the star. They were learned men seeking knowledge, wisdom, and truth. The night they knew well, and they feared neither darkness, distance, nor mystery. Perhaps, as often said, it is darkest just before the dawn. Was one of them remembering what seemed cryptic words from the scroll of some Hebrew prophet? Or was it some unfathomable spiritual transmission from an unseen power greater than any they knew upon earth, an epiphany, or a prelude to epiphany? The strange star sank low on the black western horizon, but "the sun of righteousness will rise with healing in its wings, and you will go forth...."

December 24

IMMANUEL

¹⁴ Therefore the Lord Himself will give you a sign: Behold, a virgin will be with child and bear a son, and she will call His name Immanuel.

Isaiah 7:14

The sacrificial, atoning death of our Lord Jesus Christ, followed by His resurrection from the grave, constitutes not only the essential foundation of our faith but also the single most important action in all of human history. Yet before there could be an atonement (our griefs and iniquities borne as He was pierced through for our transgressions) and before death could be conquered and life eternal made manifest as He left behind an empty tomb, there first had to be a coming. More specifically, in accordance with the divinely inspired words of the prophet, there had to be the birth of a son from the womb of a virgin. The Son of the Most High had to come down in advent to Bethlehem of Judah to dwell amongst us as one of us. The one who would be Immanuel, "God With Us," in the flesh.

The glory of His people Israel and a light of revelation to the Gentiles—we remember His coming and reflect upon it tonight, giving thanks and celebrating when morning comes. He came down to offer the forgiveness of sins and the gifts of peace and life eternal to every person. He would establish a kingdom without borders or end peopled with those of every nation, tribe, and tongue from the far corners of the earth.

Rulers, lords, and kings had come and gone for millennia just as they still do today. Likewise, nations, kingdoms, and empires had waxed and waned and risen and fallen. So continues the inexorable pattern in our own time.

The establishment of an eternal kingdom filled with men and women of every nation, tribe, and tongue was requisite of an increase of government and of peace to which there would be no end. Yet such increases of government and peace have continually and invariably proven to lay well beyond the capacities of men. Only in the coming of Immanuel, "God With Us," would there be one who, through knowledge, love, and grace, could draw all the peoples unto Himself. Only in Immanuel could there be a King of all kings, Lord of all Lords, and Prince of Peace who held the power to establish the eternal kingdom, the increase of His government and peace unimpeded.

His knowledge, unlike any heard before, would penetrate the minds and hearts of all men like a two-edged sword with timeless words of wisdom and truth. His love would define genuine love, separating affection, sentiment, lust, and emotion from the sacrificial and unconditional actions which must embody true love. Then the grace upon grace, as the disciple John phrased it, to be poured out unto all people of His fullness would let flow an irrepressible and unending river aggregating compassion, mercy, loving-kindness, gentleness, and peace in measures unknown to men. Such an aggregation never could have come from men, but only from Immanuel, "God With Us."

The distinction of *Immanuel* is not meant as the name He would commonly be called by men. The name Immanuel, rather, was to delineate who and what He was to be. He would be "God With Us," fully divine and yet wholly human, living with us as one of us. He would experience the joys, hardships, humor, burdens, challenges, suffering, pain, and sorrow of life the same as all of us. He would know us intimately, and we, Him. He would understand us but, more important, He would make Himself and the way of His Father understood by us.

Laws had been given, a covenant made and blessings bestowed, but this had proven insufficient. For by the time the strange star had been seen from far away in the East shining its light over Bethlehem of Judah, precious few remained who had been faithful to the covenant. Hearing and reading are different from seeing and experiencing. The philosopher Confucius said, "I hear, I forget; I see, I remember; I do, I understand." Immanuel was to bring the will and way of the living God into a dimension never before seen, experienced or comprehended. No longer would men only hear or read. Now they would see and experience the way of God as embodied by one who was a man just as were they.

When morning comes we celebrate then and commemorate that there was no other way for men to truly know their God and comprehend His way. Nor was there any other way, ultimately, for them to go to their God than to cross by the bridge that is the sole Mediator between God and men, the man Christ Jesus. The strife, iniquity, oppression, bloodshed, hatred, and injustice prevailing through the millennia before the advent of Immanuel established the fact that the answer and the truth lay not with men. Nearly two thousand years after Jesus' resurrection, all the same predominates still throughout the mindsets, inclinations, endeavors, and schemes of men as further evidences of that fact.

Neither perfect nor even true justice could ever be established by men. Hatred, strife, and violence have been hallmarks of man from the beginning and remain no less so today. War, far from fading amid so-called advances in technology and education, has only increased in volume as well as destructive capability. Peace has proven a slope unnegotiable and a summit insurmountable.

Yet into a world such as this Immanuel would come, and the world would never be the same as before. The ways of this world and the nature of man would not change; but the world itself, for the first and only time in history, would be changed forevermore. This change came because men, women and children were able to see the perfect embodiment of the way and love of the living God in the actions of Immanuel. Then, when He was lifted up from the earth upon a cross, He would draw all people unto Himself, just as He had promised that He would. For many would follow Him and many would reject Him. Of those who would reject Him, some would try to use intellect, persuasion or intimidation to turn minds and hearts away from Him. Others would try to drive Him away, silence Him, and, with temporary success, to kill Him. Tellingly and most revealing is the fact that those who reject Him today continue to direct the same efforts toward the millions who still follow Him.

Thus we may see more clearly all that we celebrate when morning breaks. Immanuel has drawn all people unto Himself. The disciples whom He left behind spread out across the earth and made disciples of others, and they, still others. Immanuel changed the world because, from the time He was lifted up and then risen from the dead, the embodiment of His love and way would be manifested in the lives of His true followers throughout the earth to the end.

They would embody the actions of unconditional, universal love for all people. They would feed the hungry, clothe the naked, care for the sick, treat the wounded, provide for widows and orphans, share the burdens of the downtrodden, speak truth in all things, offer forgiveness even to their enemies, seek peace with all people, and strive for genuine justice. Never would they be unopposed and always they would suffer persecution, but never would they be eliminated or stopped. For the power carried within them is that of Immanuel, "God With Us," He who neither slumbers nor sleeps and holds all authority and power in heaven and on earth.

The promise of Immanuel from the darkness of a world without Him is what we reflect upon this Christmas Eve. With the breaking of the dawn, however, we will celebrate the joy and peace brought down by "God With Us" in Jesus our Lord. We remember: The birth that changed the world, drew all people, and revealed the true thoughts of every heart came not in a palace or seat of power but in a lowly stable at the desert's edge in Bethlehem of Judah.

YOU SHALL CALL
HIS NAME JESUS

[18] Now the birth of Jesus Christ was as follows: when His mother Mary had been betrothed to Joseph, before they came together she was found to be with child by the Holy Spirit. [19] And Joseph her husband, being a righteous man and not wanting to disgrace her, planned to send her away secretly. [20] But when he had considered this, behold, an angel of the Lord appeared to him in a dream, saying, "Joseph, son of David, do not be afraid to take Mary as your wife; for the Child who has been conceived in her is of the Holy Spirit. [21] She will bear a Son; and you shall call His name Jesus, for He will save His people from their sins." [22] Now all this took place to fulfill what was spoken by the Lord through the prophet: [23] "BEHOLD, THE VIRGIN SHALL BE WITH CHILD AND SHALL BEAR A SON, AND THEY SHALL CALL HIS NAME IMMANUEL," WHICH TRANSLATED MEANS, "GOD WITH US." [24] And Joseph awoke from his sleep and did as the angel of the Lord commanded him, and took Mary as his wife, [25] but kept her a virgin until she gave birth to a Son; and he called His name Jesus.

Matthew 1:18-25

The angel said to Joseph, of Him whom we celebrate this Christmas morn: "You shall call His name Jesus, for He will save His people from their sins." Immanuel, "God With Us,' is who and what He was upon His earthly sojourn. Jesus is the name by which He was known and called and still is called upon today from the four corners of the earth in every tongue. In the more than two thousand years since His birth on that cool night in the stable in Bethlehem, His name has proven to be like no other name and the name above all names. For not only is His name still called out in adoration, praise, gratitude, and entreaty by the hundreds of millions, but by many more is called out in denial, profane exclamation, and curses. He is called out by so-called "debunkers" and called out in select justification, a process by which those who deny His claims attempt to justify a course of action by utilizing selected statements from Him, removing them from context or from the totality of His words as put forth in the four Gospels. The Bible is not the only evidence of the veracity of Jesus' boldest claim—that if He was lifted up from the earth He would draw all men to Himself (John 12:32). Rather, even two millennia later, you need only to examine the responses of men.

The name Jesus is derived from the Hebrew "Joshua," meaning "*Yahweh* saves," or "God saves." The title translated Christ is the Greek term for "anointed," thus the equivalent to the Hebrew word "Messiah." He who was born to Mary in Bethlehem was Jesus, God's anointed one, conceived of the Holy Spirit within her womb and who came in advent to save His people from their sins. He whose coming was promised by the prophets, in whose veins flowed the blameless blood of the new covenant, whose voice would restore hope amid the prophetic silence and who would shine the light of salvation unto all people in the unremitting darkness.

Neither in the millennia preceding Jesus' birth nor in those that have followed has mankind been able to establish true justice, the reign of peace, or the universal love of one for another in this temporal realm. Let alone did he have any capacity or way by which to save himself in the spiritual realm. Man knew not the way to life abundant or life everlasting, but on this day we celebrate Him who gives the gifts of abundant and everlasting life. We celebrate Him who imparts the inner peace that surpasses comprehension and the only peace that flows and remains unchanged regardless of circumstances and tribulations around us.

Life abundant comes in manifold facets to all who call upon Jesus and receive the Holy Spirit as a result of their faith and emulation of His ways. Life everlasting is bestowed upon all who call upon Him by the redemptive power of His cleansing blood as it washes away the stain of iniquity so that sins are forgiven and remembered no more. Then the peace surpassing comprehension, that which the angel and the multitude of the heavenly host declared to the shepherds in the fields outside of Bethlehem, fills and fortifies all people with whom He is pleased. The peace that comforts, calms, encourages, strengthens, and brings blessed assurance, remaining forever unchanging in an ever-changing world.

His name was to be called Jesus, "*Yahweh* Saves," because He would save us from the consequences of our sins. Yet on this Christmas day, we dwell not on the sorrow, burden, oppression, and pain brought into the world by man's sin. Rather, we celebrate the inestimable gift of the sole mediator between us and our God. As the angel declared to the shepherds, we put away fear and celebrate the "good news of great joy," which is for all people.

Because He who came in advent carried our sorrows and bore our iniquities, this day that marks His birth must be one of joy for the abundant life and love that we share together and joy in knowing that our ultimate home is not on this earth but waits and stands eternally in the heavenly place that He has gone to prepare for us. Joy is also found in the sublime, inscrutable peace that neither changes nor fades amid tempests of uncertainty, chaos, violence, destruction, oppression, or hardship. Joy arises as His peace is unchanging because He is unchanging, for "Jesus Christ is the same yesterday and today and forever" (Heb 13:8).

Embracing the joy of this Christmas day, let us affirm, in word and in actions, our love for one another. As we have been forgiven, let us be quick to forgive the trespasses of others and ready to look beyond any offense or insult. We remember the ultimate gift given freely to all in Bethlehem, so let us give freely to others of our time and our gifts, measuring our gifts not against the volume of that which may be given by others but in accordance with what God has given to each of us. Then as we feel the flow of His peace in spirit and mind, let us exude that peace toward all who enter our circles or cross our paths. Though our world be filled with conflict, hatred, and distrust, may we pursue peace with all people and among all nations. Inasmuch as it depends upon us, let us be at peace with all people. May we never take for granted the Son of God coming unto us as one of us. Let us never forget the significance of the name like no other name and name above all names, Jesus, "*Yahweh* Saves."

December 26

A STRANGE STAR AND
A NEWBORN KING

¹Now after Jesus was born in Bethlehem of Judea in the days of Herod the king, Magi from the east arrived in Jerusalem, saying, ² "Where is He who has been born King of the Jews? For we saw His star in the east and have come to worship Him."

Matthew 2:1-2

The Nonconformist biblical exegete and Presbyterian minister at Chester, Matthew Henry, made this observation; "Those who live at the greatest distance from the means of grace often use most diligence, and learn to know the most about Christ and His salvation." Of the strange star that drew the Magi from far in the east, Joseph Hall, Bishop of Exeter and then of Norwich, wrote, "It is the goodness of God, that, in those means wherein we cannot reach Him, He descends unto us." Both observations are pertinent as we reflect upon the quest of the Magi and the significance thereof both for each individual and for the Gospel of Jesus Christ in full.

Despite the errant musings of Augustine and Tertullian, the Magi were never kings. The makers, counselors, or influencers of kings they may have been, but never kings or rulers. The Greek gentleman soldier and writer Xenophon, having had some exposure to them, classified the Magi as being the authorities in all religious matters. He further speculated that they might have been responsible for the education of the young emperor-to-be, which, at least in certain periods, may have been true.

What we can know for certain is that the Magi were men of great influence who were respected and probably revered by most within their realm. Being Zoroastrian priests, they were the religious leaders of the religion of the prophet Zoroaster. They believed in a deity by the name of Ahura Mazda, the creator and sole god of the universe. Meticulous observers and charters of the night sky, no men anywhere knew the stars, constellations, planets, and nocturnal movements better. Assertions of varied esoteric knowledge and abilities within the field of magic have been common through the ages. The foremost astronomers of their time, the Magi were also renowned astrologers, as they sought in the presence, formations, and movements of the celestial bodies spiritual truths, temporal understandings, and prophecies. Though not rulers, the esteem in which they were held and the fact that they were considered to be the possessors of certain knowledge, wisdom, and understanding beyond even the capacities of great kings or the noble elite, insured that they remained men of power and influence who probably lacked for nothing in terms of sustenance and material goods.

All the above, the much we still do not know, and the substantial distance between Persia and Israel—geographical and religious—combine to render the Magi the most mysterious and intriguing characters to appear in the story of Jesus' birth. While we can presume most, at least, of the above to have been true of the particular Magi to whom we are introduced in Matthew's Gospel, we learn more of significance about them from these opening verses of chapter two. Concerning the number of Magi making the journey, we are given something but left with a lingering question. That there were at least two men is clear. Tradition has held that there were three Magi based upon the presentation of three gifts. The number of gifts brought, however, verifies nothing regarding the number of men. There may have been three but there could have been ten, twenty, thirty or more. Though a smaller number may seem more likely, on this side of Heaven we will probably never know.

Though we are not told this, we can infer the probability that the Magi who came before Herod had some familiarity with Hebrew Scripture. A presence of Jews in Persia was established at some point not long after the Babylonian captivity. The Babylonians carried out three major deportations of Jews—in 597 B.C., 587 B.C., and then in 582 B.C. Following his conquest of Babylon, the Persian king, Cyrus the Great, founder of the Achaemenid Empire, freed the Jews there and allowed all who wished to return to Jerusalem to begin rebuilding the temple, which was commenced in 537 B.C. Many Jews, however, remained in Persian-controlled Babylon or moved further east into Persia proper where there soon developed a well-established and growing Jewish community. Though the Jews in the east were comfortable there and proved themselves adaptable in culture and business, they brought with them their Scripture and their rabbis. Magi, being scholars and seekers of knowledge and possessed with an inherent intellectual curiosity, likely read some of the Hebrew scrolls of Scripture and heard or conversed with the rabbis on matters religious, theological, and spiritual. Without at all diminishing the revelation of the epiphany, the knowledge of the Jews, their homeland, and of a newborn king suggest some awareness of the tenets and prophecies of Judaism.

Most interesting and more important, verse two establishes the nature and purpose of the Magi's quest. Modern historians who even acknowledge the possibility of the truth of the Magi's visit, predictably, have tried to write any spiritual or religious connotation out of the account. This conclusion is based upon what they wish to be true and what they wish to persuade others of rather than upon the demonstrable truth that is as readily clear in the text as it is in the simple process of reason.

"Where is He who has been born King of the Jews? For we saw His star in the east and have come to worship Him." To the point of reason, note that the Magi knew well that the man to whom they addressed this question ruled absolutely in civil and military affairs as the king of the Jews in all of Roman Palestine. The king whom they sought had just been born and, as they would have realized, was not a member of this ruling family. Thus they sought an infant or a child with no apparent royal blood, a fact that rules out any assertion that this visit was some type of diplomatic gesture or political mission. Just to note the obvious, no attempt at diplomacy would begin by asking a reigning king where the true king of his people, who had just been born, could be found, and a child not even of that king's own blood no less. Furthermore, neither the Magi nor the Parthian Empire wanted or needed anything from Herod. After a couple centuries of inconclusive battles, the Parthians were content to have Herod's benign little kingdom as a buffer on the frontier between them and the eastern fringe of the Roman Empire. The Magi's quest was clearly apolitical, and equally apparent is the fact that the king they sought could not have been a king in the way that the world determined kings.

Their final words verify the nature of their search and make plain their purpose. "We saw His star in the east and have come to worship Him." Many theories have been put forth regarding the nature of the star. Whether the star was one created and shown just for the purpose of being the Magi's guiding light, was a naturally occurring but unique phenomenon dictated by the forces of nature already set in motion by our Creator's hand and manifested then and there for His purposes, or the planet Venus (as recently proposed by at least a couple scholars due to what would have been its nighttime location and connection with Rome and, thus, a king in a Roman province), matters not. The searching and tracking of stars and planets were a component of the Magi's religious practice. That they associated their quest for the newborn king with their searching of the stars suggests a spiritual quest. That they referred to the star as "His star" confirms their belief that the king they sought had power, domain, and purpose beyond the temporal realm of earthly expectations and ways. Their quest was solely spiritual.

Their purpose was stated as concisely as it was lucidly. They had "come to worship Him." The Magi did not worship kings, neither their own king nor kings of other lands. They did not worship even Zoroaster himself. Yet they sought this newborn King, seemingly unknown to everyone and even to His own people in His own land, so they could worship Him. They came to worship this unknown King, apparently without royal lineage or blood, lacking land, palaces, fortifications, armies, or attendants. What they sought was not of the temporal realm but of the spiritual, and their goal "to worship Him" was wholly spiritual.

With respect to the Church Fathers, this is why it is suggested that the Magi's epiphany could not have commenced upon their encounter with Jesus. Their epiphany had been made manifest to them before they even left their Persian homeland. For they demonstrated understanding of the spiritual nature and purpose of the King they were seeking and of the fact that His kingdom had to be of a kind unknown to, and unrecognized by, men. No other king had "His star," and we find no other king deemed by Magi to be worthy of worship. Their epiphany may have been enhanced or expanded upon their eventual meeting with Jesus, Joseph, and Mary; or perhaps we could say that it was completed or made fully manifest then. Yet the epiphany they received while still far away in Persia, in conjunction with whatever knowledge they had of Hebrew Scripture, produced an astonishingly accurate understanding of what was to be the nature and domain of the newborn King of the Jews. Noteworthy, too, is the fact that the Magi's discernment of the nature and domain of the King revealed in their epiphany far exceeded the understanding of most Jews regarding the same in their expectation of the Messiah. For the Jews envisioned a king in the mold of David, but greater than David, who would wield political and military power in addition to restoring religious fidelity.

There is a final aspect of the mindset and quest of the Magi subtly revealed in these verses. They were Zoroastrian priests faithful in the service of Ahura Mazda, whom they believed to be the lone creator and god. Yet they sought a newborn king of another people and faith whose domain could only be a spiritual one. For however humble His circumstances and whatever He lacked of the requisites of earthly power, they sought to worship Him. Somehow, at some point within the confluence of their epiphany and their ceaseless seeking and study, they became aware of a fissure in the longstanding house of Zoroaster.

They felt a void left unfilled by doctrine and explanations to which they had faithfully adhered. Not only a void in Zoroastrianism, but in all doctrines and explanations within religions and philosophies of men that they had long searched out and contemplated. None else can explain the quest, the journey toward the star, to seek out a newborn king whose kingdom could only be a spiritual one. A king unlike any other and worthy of worship, and a king in whose kingdom seemingly men of every nation and tongue would be welcomed. The king they sought would hold a power unprecedented and unfathomable. He would issue counsel never before heard. He would answer questions that had silenced men or reduced them to fantasied ramblings.

Those to whom truth has been given often become dulled to the power and resonance of truth. Those living closest to the means of grace, who have received grace and who have seen the blessings of the grace upon grace of Jesus Christ manifested all around them can easily succumb to the error of taking that grace for granted. Thus they fail to appreciate the magnitude and necessity of grace to the human condition. When they fail to appreciate, they will fail to act accordingly in response.

Yet those living at the greatest distance from the means of grace often seek with greater diligence and will learn to know the most of Christ and His salvation. Those who have walked the path of darkness in search of the light of truth will not merely look askance at the appearance of a strange star that beckons. Nor will they be put off by any distance to be traversed or hardship to be endured to discover what its light may reveal beyond the black horizon. Those who have understood the ultimate emptiness of the pursuit of material things and temporal gain will not be content with such pursuits. Nor will they hesitate to search out that which looks beyond the temporal to the timeless and eternal. Those who have seen the rising and falling of kings and kingdoms and understand the fragility of life and futility of all human endeavor will not balk at seeking out a king who dwells not in a palace and whose kingdom is not marked by walls, land, and borders. Those who realize the ends of sin and know the hopelessness of the absence of grace will stop at nothing to pursue the promise of unbounded grace.

Geographically and spiritually, the Magi who came before Herod lived far from the means of grace. Yet because of their great distance from grace, so much more did they understand and appreciate the magnitude of grace. Knowing the utter futility of human endeavor and the plans of kings and kingdoms, so much more did they yearn to bow before the King whose kingdom was not to be of their world. Harboring a void of soul that lingered still after decades of study, searching and religious devotion, they would follow the star to the ends of the earth to find the knowledge, grace, and peace that only could fill that emptiness.

Such was the disposition and commitment of the Magi, but when dwelling far away from the source of knowledge and means of grace, commitment and great effort may not be sufficient. When people in any time and place seek truth with all that is within them and with minds and hearts fully open, however, our God has shown time and again that, in one way or another, He will descend to them and make Himself and His will known. So did He descend to the Magi who sought ultimate truth by all means available to them, using the light of a star or some celestial body, which they were certain to investigate. Note that God did not reveal all things to them. Considered against the totality of all mystery, He actually revealed very little, and He does not reveal the answers to all questions to any person. Jesus did not even do so for the twelve disciples chosen as His closest companions. What our Lord will do is to descend to us, meet us somewhere upon the path of our wholehearted search, and grant us His peace and the knowledge of the way to salvation.

The search of the Magi He met in a place they knew very well—the night sky. He gave to them an epiphany of extraordinary understanding. Then the guidance of His star took them, literally, to the face of God in His Son Jesus, the way, the truth and the life abundant and everlasting. Whether we live near or far from the manifestations of His grace, let us never take that grace for granted. Let us never cease to be amazed, inspired, and grateful. Even when we have found Him and received the gift of His salvation, may we ne'er stop seeking His way and striving after righteousness. Then whether seeking salvation, answers, or a guiding light, let us remember that if our own efforts have been exhausted and our abilities can advance us no more, He will then descend unto us with His "star" to guide us the rest of the way. Just as the Magi, we must seek and complete our journey; but we do not go alone, for He goes with us each step of the way.

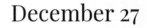

December 27

HEROD'S TROUBLES

> *³ When Herod the king heard this, he was troubled, and all Jerusalem with him.*
>
> Matthew 2:3

While asserting a valid point, Matthew's statement in verse three is not without humor. As prone as the paranoid king was to extended fits of violent rage, when Herod was troubled, all around him were troubled also, in Jerusalem and often beyond. But what was the primary source of Herod's troubles? The presumed and universally accepted answer has been that it was the news from the Magi that a new King of the Jews had just been born somewhere in Herod's domain. Herod was a man who would not tolerate even the prospect of a rival to his throne, either from within or outside of his family. He had killed three of his own sons, his seventeen-year-old brother-in-law, and his favorite wife Miriamne, essentially for that reason, and he had killed others for less. Paranoid and ruthless though he was, however, Herod was intelligent and savvy to the realities of the world. At his age and in his situation, he would not have felt genuinely threatened by reports that a baby born to unknown parents was being announced as "King of the Jews." He would have followed up on the report and taken violent action so as to end any such talk or speculation just as he eventually did in Bethlehem, but he would not have felt threatened in the way he had with older potential rivals already holding some standing.

Given what is known of Herod's own methods and thinking, surely it could have crossed his mind that the neighboring Parthian Empire to the east intended to utilize this supposed infant king as a mere puppet ruler. Through him, they would become the de facto rulers of Herod's kingdom of Judea, putting them into position by some greater scheme to remove the Herodian dynasty and ultimately to push Rome and her influence out of the Levant once and for all. Yet Herod knew well that he had a powerful ally in Rome and that the Parthians, despite immense efforts over many years, had never been able to push Rome completely off the Asian continent. Such a scheme, if indeed Herod thought of it, likely would have seemed a long shot at best. An irritation, to be sure, but hardly an imminent threat to his rule.

Merely a report of some unknown infant king could never have driven him to the extremes of paranoia and rage that soon followed. For a part of Matthew's humor is that, if we judge solely by specific wording, he actually understated the fact. In truth, Herod was beyond being merely troubled, which when taking the entirety of Matthew's passage in context is readily evidenced.

Already terminally paranoid and with the arrival of the Magi, Herod quickly spiraled into a seething rage fueled by an odd combination of anger, confusion, anxiety, fear, and helplessness. Too, at the moment, he had no outlet for this rage. There were no targets he could afford to hit so as to assuage the violent impulses. Though it may seem incongruous to suggest fear and helplessness as contributing factors to the state of an absolute monarch whose kingdom and throne face no credible threat, they irrefutably were significant in pushing him even closer to the brink of madness and, thus, perhaps even a bit closer to his soon-to-come date with eternal destiny.

Before examining the scope of Herod's troubles, though, let us complete as accurate a perspective on the visiting Magi as is possible. The view perceived by most regarding these mysterious travelers from the East is greatly influenced by countless artistic depictions, nativity scenes, Church tradition, and Sunday school lessons and sermons. All this is good, contributing much to the joy of Christmas, but it may leave something to be desired for those in search of an accurate historical perspective. While the number of Magi making the trip remains in question, so, too, does the number of those who undoubtedly accompanied them. To imagine that two, three, or ten priests of high standing set out to cross a large swath of western Asia alone and unarmed while bearing gifts and possessions of great monetary value would be as naïve as it is unthinkable. The Magi were wise men, and no wise men with a choice would have considered such an undertaking in that time and place. Recall that Jesus Himself, when preparing His disciples and closest followers to carry the gospel out into all the world after He was gone, commanded that they possess swords and sell their coats in order to buy swords if they did not have them already (Luke 22:36). Better, according to our Lord Jesus, to be coatless and cold than warm and unarmed!

Whatever the actual number of Magi, their party riding up to Herod's gate was a large one, heavily armed and formidable. Whether they rode horses or camels cannot be known, but their choice would have depended, in part, upon the route by which they had planned to travel. That both animals were utilized is possible and, based upon the capacities, strengths, and weaknesses of each, seems probable.

The largest segment of the Magi party, especially if the number of Magi themselves was relatively small, was probably their military escort. With the influence of church tradition and artistic depictions, some may be surprised or uneasy with such a notion. The assertion, nevertheless, is now supported by some of the foremost scholars in the field. The reason for this scholarly consensus is clear. While we have no record of specific detail in this case, all that we do know of ancient Persia and the greater region would suggest a formidable presence around the Magi. The same is inferred with the simplest application of logic.

The Magi, being respected and esteemed throughout Persia and in much of the Parthian Empire, were important men who would have been deemed worthy of protection. Furthermore, whether wealthy or not and whether they lived simply or extravagantly, they were men, at least, with access to resources. Their military guard could have been Parthian cavalry. Persian cavalry, by this point in time, had long been established as one of the most effective and lethal mounted forces the world had known. Outnumbered nearly four to one by the Roman Triumvir Crassus and his seven legions at Carrhae in 53 B.C., a Parthian cavalry force had handed Rome one of the worst and most humiliating defeats in her long history. Also possibly, the Magi's escort was a mercenary cavalry unit selected for specific skills and/or knowledge of lands to be crossed. In either case, the gleaming blades of spearheads on cherry wood shafts, bows, quivers of arrows, and shamshirs on cavalrymen mounted on fine Persian or Median horses would have been prominent.

Formidable as the force would have appeared, however, they would not have been provocative. To the contrary, they would have strictly adhered to all military and diplomatic protocol regarding peaceful missions between nations. Their role was simply to put forth a silent statement that the Magi were not to be harassed, trifled with, or impeded. They would neither have spoken nor drawn weapons unless life or property was threatened.

The reasons for the presence of such a guard are readily apparent. Between the gold, frankincense, and myrrh and some of the finest livestock on the continent, the monetary value with which they rode was substantial. Crossing vast fringes of empires and a frontier sparsely inhabited in places, well-armed bandits who knew the land far better than did they were a significant threat. Lions, leopards, hyenas, and wolves—prevalent throughout the Ancient Near East and especially prone to attacking resting livestock or humans in the dead of night—had to be expected. Though they likely did not expect any challenge from Herod or from the Romans, they would be entering the territory of both. As the Magi were revered men of high standing, Parthian authorities would be inclined to send a polite, silent message that any attack or affront upon them would be taken seriously.

So we return to the source of Herod's trouble, which was not, as is commonly presumed, the birth of Jesus. The presence in his kingdom of a newborn baby said by foreigners to be the King of the Jews would have struck Herod as an annoyance rather than a threat, an irritation upon which he would act but hardly a serious threat to his dynasty. The source of Herod's trouble was the Magi themselves. The mere appearance of Magi from the Parthian Empire in his court, before even a word had been said, instantly turned Herod's world upside down and sent his mind into a raging tailspin. Their reason for coming mattered not, for the damage was done and a snare was laid in an instant. Such a party, dressed in fine and obviously foreign clothing, with impressive animals and guarded by a small but potent cavalry force could not go unnoticed. Nor were they likely to be kept a secret. How many people had seen them ride through

Jerusalem and up to Herod's palace? How many saw them enter, or saw Parthian soldiers, horses, camels, and baggage waiting outside?

Though Herod ruled his kingdom absolutely, he did so only at the pleasure of Caesar Augustus in Rome. If Augustus found out that Herod had met with any kind of high-ranking delegation from the Parthian Empire, and Herod could not conceive of any way the Emperor would not eventually hear of it, then he was going to be furious. He would immediately suspect Herod in some way of plotting or collaborating with the Parthians against Rome's interests. Though the two empires had settled into a grudging peace, the Parthian Empire still was Rome's most formidable enemy and competitor. The Parthians had spilled substantial amounts of Roman blood, handed Rome one of her most humiliating defeats, and stilled her schemes of eastward expansion. Augustus did not want another war, but nor did he want any ruler in one of his provinces to have dealings with the Parthians without his knowledge and permission.

Furthermore, under Augustus' rule, Rome had enjoyed an unprecedented era of prosperity. Materials and luxury goods flowed in from all over Europe, Africa, and from as far east as China. Interestingly, Chinese records state that a Roman embassy, coming by way of Jiaozhi in northern Vietnam, entered the Han capital of Luoyang in A.D.166 during the reigns of Emperor Marcus Aurelius in Rome and Emperor Huan in Han China. Roman gold jewelry from the Antonine period (A.D. 96—A.D. 192) and gold medallions dating to the reigns of Antonine Pius and Marcus Aurelius have been discovered at Oc Eo on the Mekong Delta in southern Vietnam. All goods coming into Rome from China or India came via the Silk Road, a lengthy stretch of which ran through the Parthian Empire. Rome wished for the road to remain open, merchandise to flow, and trade to flourish. Thus the last thing Augustus wanted was a conflict that could deplete his own treasury while impeding commerce. Whatever Augustus did not want, Herod knew that he also could not want, let alone have any part at all, unintended or not, in bringing about.

So, Herod's serious and immediate trouble lay to the west, his mind spinning desperately in search of some explanation. How could he explain to Augustus? Tell him that they were just religious men searching for a newborn child whom they said was the King of the Jews? The emperor surely was not going to believe that. For that matter, no one who had not actually heard the Magi's words for themselves was going to believe that.

Then to the east lay the potential for great trouble and trouble that, if initiated, was sure to bring down the wrath of Augustus from the west. While Herod wanted the Magi gone and out of his country immediately, he could not afford to say so. Let alone could he lift a hand against them or even threaten to do so. Any perceived insult or any act of force put him at risk of hostilities with the Parthian Empire, against whom he could never hold his own if it came to war. Yet the fact hardly mattered. For any conflict with the Parthians would bring in Augustus' legions and the probable end both of Herod's rule and his independent kingdom.

Herod had troubles of a kind that he could not have seen coming and a problem he never could have even imagined. His status and that of his kingdom was suddenly at risk, not because of some so-called newborn King of the Jews, but because of the appearance of Magi and their entourage in his court. As the all-powerful ruler of his kingdom, for the first time in his long reign he faced a threat against which he was powerless to act. Any action he took was likely to bring trouble. Inaction, likewise, could bring trouble. To make matters worse, the nature of the Magi's stated mission suggested that they would be remaining in the country for at least a few days, thus being seen by more eyes and talked about by more mouths. Herod's fear arose, his rage intensified, and his ever-present paranoia deepened for this reason. Yet with all this building and burning within him, the king had no target he could strike by which his rage might be expunged. Thus, the previous suggestion of the possibility, at least, that the arrival of the Magi might have taken a few months, or years, off the troubled king's life. For Herod was desperately troubled, and all Jerusalem, and soon to be Bethlehem, with him.

What is to be understood and reflected upon in Herod's troubles are the mysterious and manifold ways of the workings of our God. Living, active, and never slumbering, He works and accomplishes His will through all kinds of people in every type of situation and circumstance. Here, at once, we see that He accomplished multiple facets of His will and plan, working, on the one hand, through devout men of faith with open hearts and minds and, on the other, through a wicked man driven by the demonic and by the sole obsession of his own earthly power and glory. On the fringes of the two great empires and unbeknownst to both, He used the presence and powers of both toward His ends.

The ways and ends of our Lord often are not clearly manifested to human understanding for years, decades, centuries, or even millennia after He has moved. Some of those ends and ways may forever remain a mystery. Yet always He is working, and always in ways, places, events, and through people whom most would not expect.

Too, understand and reflect upon the difference between sight and perception. The great swordsman, Musashi, wrote and cautioned his disciples that sight is weak while perception is strong. Similarly, and for the same reason, Scripture commands us not to walk by sight but rather by faith, and true perception is one of the components of faith.

Things, situations, and people are often quite different from the mere image available to the eyes. If a man never saw anything of the ocean except for the frequently rough surface of the North Atlantic, he would actually know very little about the sea. His vision could be 20/20 and his mind sharp, but his perception would be greatly flawed.

In accordance with the sight of men looking upon outward things, Herod had it all: unlimited possessions, luxury, opulent surroundings, security, and absolute power. In short, all those things that can bring one contentment, peace, and happiness. Yet now we know that Herod's spirit and mind were never at peace and that happiness eluded him, especially in his later years as the paranoia, bitterness, rage, and the conscience of bloodshed did their nefarious work within him. Further, in retrospect we realize the absolute ruler discovered the limits of his power even within his own small kingdom. Many saw, but very few perceived.

The Magi, conversely, could have appeared ridiculous to the eyes. Grown men with power, wealth, and prestige leaving their homes in one of the earth's greatest nations and superpowers and traveling far to bow down and worship the unknown child of parents without pedigree or rank in a town unknown beyond its region. Now, however, just as with the life of Herod, we know the end of the Magi's story and of the story of Him before whom they bowed down and worshipped. Being wise men, the Magi had not interpreted their epiphany or embarked upon their long search based upon sight. Nor did they bow down before Jesus and bestow upon Him their gifts because of what was seen. They understood well that appearances were deceptive and sight was weak. What they perceived, though, at depths below and beyond the range of the eyes, was something miraculous, unprecedented, truly beautiful, and desperately needed in the human soul.

December 28

BETHLEHEM OF JUDEA

> *⁴ Gathering together all the chief priests and scribes of the people, he inquired of them where the Messiah was to be born. ⁵ They said to him, "In Bethlehem of Judea; for this is what has been written by the prophet: ⁶ 'And you, Bethlehem, land of Judah, Are by no means least among the leaders of Judah; For out of you shall come forth a Ruler Who will shepherd My people Israel.'"*

> Matthew 2:4-6

E ven with only a rudimentary knowledge of Scripture, you cannot think of Jesus—Messiah, Christ and Savior for all people—and not remember Bethlehem. The Advent of the Son of the living God born as one of us to be fully human and still wholly divine cannot be considered apart from the location and circumstances of His birth. Not when both location and circumstances, to human eyes and thought, would seem to have so little to commend them. Bethlehem

Ephratha was noted by Micah as "too little to be among the clans of Judah," thus a town considered to be without significance even by those dwelling within and around it.

Yet in this little town a ruler and shepherd for all of Israel was to be born. Though born a helpless babe in a cave and makeshift stable at the town's edge, the prophet notes that "His goings forth are from long ago, from the days of eternity." A difficult concept for many in and of itself, how much more then does it beg the questions? Why a birth at all, but surely, why in Bethlehem?

The answer to the question of "Why a birth?" could seem sufficiently simple for any who have deeply pondered the ceaseless bloodshed, injustice, greed, depravity, and oppression that has been the hallmark of man through the millennia. For peace, perfect justice, universal empathy, and love for our fellow man has proven beyond human ability just as much as it is beyond the capacities to control courses of nature, the ravaging march of time, and the surety of death. The question of "Why Bethlehem?" however, may prove unanswerable to any quorum on our side of eternity. Many, nevertheless, have felt inclined to ask, seeking understanding and answer.

While the significance of the choice and location of Bethlehem, including the question of whether or not there is significance at all, can surely be disputed, the impact of the most celebrated birth in Bethlehem's long history remains indisputable. Time itself, as we mark and measure it, hinges upon Bethlehem. We denote the many years before the Advent of Jesus Christ as B.C. and then mark the years after His birth in Bethlehem as A.D.—anno Domini, the year of our Lord. In the relatively new and increasingly frequent use of B.C.E. (Before the Common Era) and C.E. (Common Era) can be seen a dichotomous acknowledgement of the centrality and inescapable draw of Bethlehem. For every person who writes or speaks the letters B.C.E. or C.E. is fully cognizant of his desire and determination to avoid acknowledging or speaking the name of Jesus Christ. This reality, however, should never be troubling to believers, because such desire and determination, in and of itself, constitutes arguably the rawest and most sincere form of acknowledgement. Bethlehem weighs heavier in the minds of those willfully trying to avoid acknowledgement than it does in the minds of many believers who speak, read, or write the letters B.C. and A.D. with scarcely a passing thought regarding the magnitude of their significance.

In it all could be suggested a pertinent question for the erudite scholars of academia. What, precisely, became so "common" in the year A.D. 1 and has remained so to our present day that was not "common" through the millennia of the era before? What shook the world between 1 B.C. and A.D. 1 so much that a central point was established from which time would be forever marked and measured?

Those who are His own and walk in His way know well the life-changing and world-changing power that came down in Advent in Bethlehem. They know the inner peace that surpasses all comprehension and something of the depths of genuine love. They realize the impact of grace and that of the unparalleled blessing of the grace upon grace poured out in Christ. They know why all of time hinges on Bethlehem. And not only time but all of life, every act and endeavor of men under the sun, and the ultimate destination of each immortal soul to have held the breath of life upon this earth – all hinge upon Bethlehem. For as we are told at the opening of John's gospel, "He was in the beginning with God. All things came into being through Him, and apart from Him nothing came into being that has come into being. In Him was life, and the life was the Light of men."

Yet it was to Bethlehem that He came down, and there that men and women would first look into His eyes and worship Him. Still we can wonder, why Bethlehem?

What we know of the way taught and embodied by Jesus might tempt us toward a conclusion that it was Bethlehem's insignificance that drew Him there. For He clearly had no interest in occupying the grand palaces of Jerusalem, Rome, Ecbatana, or Susa. In His own words, "the Son of Man did not come to be served, but to serve, and to give His life a ransom for many." In some cases, though, one must be wary of easy answers. Is there more to Bethlehem than meets the eye or cursory thought?

Perhaps the greatest love story in all Scripture played out in Bethlehem. Boaz, acting as kinsman-redeemer, took the Moabite widow Ruth as his own wife, securing both her and her mother-in-law Naomi for life. Therein, of course, is foreshadowed the coming of Jesus, the ultimate Kinsman-Redeemer, our brother as a man and our redeemer unto life eternal as the Son of God who willingly spilled His lifeblood on behalf of all people.

Israel's greatest warrior and king, the great-grandson of Ruth, also came from Bethlehem. It was to be his throne, according to the angel Gabriel's message to Mary, that Jesus would be given. "He will be great and will be called the Son of the Most High; and the Lord God will give Him the throne of His father David." What then, if anything, is special about Bethlehem?

Six miles south of Jerusalem, Bethlehem rests at almost 2600 feet in the southern end of the Judean Hills, nearly 100 feet higher than Jerusalem. Some of the surrounding hills rise to 3000 feet. Contrary to presumptions in the West, Bethlehem is not desert. Rather, the town sits at the desert's edge, where the drop-off and contrast of the Judean Wilderness is readily visible and dramatic. Bethlehem and its surrounding hills, however, have long yielded a remarkable variety and quantity of produce. Wheat and barley grow well there. Thus the Hebrew name for Bethlehem, *Bet Lehem*, "house of bread." There is abundant grazing for livestock in the hills, especially after the winter rains and into the spring. Thus the constant presence of shepherds even today and the Arabic name, *Bayt Laham*, "house of meat." In addition to grain and livestock, olives, figs, apricots, grapes, and almonds grow in abundance. Citrus trees, though a later introduction, also do well there. Such a rich agricultural output is possible for two reasons. First, in contrast to the Judean Desert to the east and south, Bethlehem's climate is moderated by altitude and so is protected from damaging extremes of heat or cold. Even on the hotter days, the sea breeze off the Mediterranean can usually be felt by around noon. Second, within the limestone layers beneath the town lays a substantial aquifer, which fed many springs in the surrounding area and sustained the fruit trees in what used to be extensive orchards.

Bethlehem's abundant waters not only sustained its substantial harvests but, in time, were required to sustain Jerusalem's ever-growing population. During Seleucid rule around 200 B.C., the Greeks built an aqueduct that carried water from Bethlehem down to Jerusalem. Herod the Great later improved upon that with a second aqueduct built in the Roman style. Thus from a military point of view, Bethlehem has long been a key to controlling Jerusalem. Whoever controlled the water held the upper hand, and so it has played out many times in conflicts since the building of the two aqueducts.

Bethlehem's delicious and distinct olive oil has long been known. A regular trade route to Egypt was opened well over three thousand years ago. Running south through Hebron and then descending the Judean Hills into the Negev Desert, the road passed through Beersheba, the Sinai Desert, and then into the Nile Valley where the jars of olive oil were sold among the wealthier of the Egyptian populace.

Bethlehem sits on the trade route that came up from the Dead Sea and split leading west into Gaza and Jaffa. Dead

51

Sea cosmetics, though having grown in popularity worldwide in recent decades, are not a new enterprise. The utilization and marketing of chemicals and minerals derived therefrom were well established long before the birth of Jesus. Alum from the Dead Sea, for example, was commonly used as an astringent in the cosmetics of the ancient Near East. Due to proximity, Bethlehem became a center for processes related to the utilization of Dead Sea chemicals.

Its position at the edge of the great deserts to the east and south—stretching into Arabia and connecting with Africa—and an abundance of water and food put Bethlehem on the route of other traders and caravanners. Frankincense from Dhofar (modern Oman), the Hadhramaut, and Sheba (Yemen), myrrh from Sheba and Punt (Somalia), gold from Arabia, ivory and gold from East Africa and varied seashells from the Indian Ocean are among the products to pass through Bethlehem in the extensive caravan trade. Inevitably, the movement of goods from such diverse and faraway places made Bethlehem a crossroad of an ever-shifting variegation of peoples.

Just to the south of town lay some of the best stone quarries in all of Palestine. These quarries were both heavily utilized and closely guarded by Rome's Tenth Legion in the years surrounding Jesus' birth. The presence of the Tenth Legion, in fact, is indicative of another longstanding reality. Bethlehem, despite its diminutive stature, has been heavily militarized since well before Roman presence, and it remains so to this day. From the earliest days this was for the purpose of protecting Jerusalem's water supply. While guarding the miles of aqueducts was paramount among the Tenth Legion's duties, it also was tasked with policing the desert frontier of Rome's border with Parthia, protecting livestock from nomadic desert raiders who roamed comfortably up to the town's eastern edge, securing the Dead Sea chemicals trade, and eventually guarding Herod's summer palace (the

Herodium) to the southeast as well as the stone quarries so vital to the king's constant building projects.

Bethlehem, in every era, has been a town beset by a certain tension. Such a tension, while surely being more palpable at some times than at others was, nevertheless, inherently and unavoidably there. Always there have been innate, inevitable levels of distrust, suspicion, and wariness between the sedentary dwellers in cities and the nomadic peoples skilled at arms, highly mobile, and constantly on the move in the desert outside the city walls.

This natural tension between sedentary and nomadic peoples is referenced in the description of Ishmael given by the angel in Genesis 16:12. "His hand will be against everyone and everyone's hand will be against him." This statement was not, as is too often taken, a prophecy that Ishmael and his descendants were to be a nation of misanthropes or were to be constantly at war with the people of the covenant. Rather, the angel's statement was simply an acknowledgement of the age-old reality that there is always some level of tension between the settled and the nomadic. Ishmael was to roam far and wide as a nomad in the Arabian Desert. While there always have been periods of open hostility between the two, more often than not there was peace and even varying levels of interaction. Some level of suspicion and wariness, though, has forever been the rule. As for Ishmael and Isaac, there is no indication in Scripture of anything but peace between them. They buried their father together, in peace, in the cave of Machpelah.

As for Bethlehem, what should begin to be clear is that all within its course and condition through the ages has been determined by location. Altitude and rich aquifers make possible the sustained, abundant harvests of fruits, nuts, and grains and the sustenance for livestock. Ample waters also have drawn a continual military presence. The nearby stone quarries, aside from providing a plentitude of solid building material, were also sure to draw political and military attention in time. Being positioned at the desert's edge guaranteed that there would be the inherent tension between settled people and the nomads just beyond the gate. Interestingly, and despite the mutual wariness, the relationship between the two always had a symbiotic side to it. The town dwellers needed the meat, wool, and leather that came from the nomad's flocks. The nomads needed markets in which to sell their livestock or trade for produce of the orchards and fields or for products made in the cities. That Bethlehem held a position essentially straddling an unmarked line between two worlds insured that such a symbiosis was easily possible and was, in fact, the norm.

Finally, being perfectly positioned for ample food, water, and commerce in a moderate climate on the only land bridge connecting Africa, Asia, and Europe assured the passing through of traders and caravans with goods manifold and diverse from near and far away. A variety of merchandise, in turn, meant the passing and coming together of different peoples with differing ways, appearances, beliefs, and tongues. Diminutive and remote, Bethlehem may have been, but location alone would be sufficient to assure it would never be ignored.

Yet only one event could have made the little town of Bethlehem known to all the world. Just one occurrence could have caused that name to be uttered in a thousand tongues in every nation of the world, as well as being remembered, celebrated, and cherished by billions. Solely one phenomenon would seal her immortality, ensuring her name and old, old story would be passed down to every new generation and that people from every land would flock to her in unprecedented numbers.

That event, a phenomenon of heaven and earth, was the birth of Jesus Christ, only begotten Son of the living God and the Savior for all people. Having neither title, estate, status, wealth, army, nor weapons, in time He drew all men unto Himself so that even all of time itself would hinge upon Him and thus upon Bethlehem where shepherds and Magi first bowed in worship at Advent. Still we are left with the question, "Why Bethlehem?" An answer to satisfy all, of course, is unlikely to be found, but perhaps even an inadequate attempt to approach some answer can render a thought or two worthy of reflection.

For Bethlehem, whence came our Lord, though "too little to be among the clans of Judah," could be seen as but a microcosm of the greater world which He came to save. Bethlehem was a place of commerce, with constant buying, selling, trading, bargaining, and the making of deals. Since the dawn of civilization, and with the possible exceptions of oppression and war, it could be argued that no single pursuit has better or more universally defined man than the ever-present mercantilism and commerce. To buy, sell, acquire, expand, build and to possess and gain still more has proven an innate human drive seldom even eased or slackened by onsets of the surety of mortality.

Bethlehem, though remote and far from seats of power, was known to generals and kings. The foremost symbol of national power—a dominant army—was seldom far from the town. At the time of Jesus' birth, in addition to King Herod's own soldiers, it was Caesar's formidable Tenth Legion that resided there. In our present day, a well-armed Palestinian militia knows that the overwhelming power of the Israel Defense Forces waits close behind the wall. As previously noted, conflict, weapons, and war have characterized men and nations as much as has commerce and markets.

Tension, too, has forever been a defining characteristic of men and nations. Fed by mutual distrust, suspicion, greed, hatred, fear, and misunderstanding, you need not look far in the streets or headlines to realize that the tensions in this world are waxing rather than waning. Sitting astride a boundary between two worlds, the settled and the nomadic, the Bethlehem into which Jesus was born was possessed of a natural tension. Bethlehem of today is no less so, even if for different reasons.

Yet Jesus came down into a town and world of tension and strife to walk in peace and embody love. Like Bethlehem, He too stood on a line between two worlds—the material and temporal on one side and the divine and eternal on the other. Just as there was a necessary connection between the sedentary world of the townspeople and that of the far-ranging nomads so, too, He revealed that there was an inherent and ineludible connection between the temporal and eternal. Man himself walked a line between two worlds and two opposing forces, the divine and the spiritual forces of wickedness.

Because His will was that all would see a better way to live amid the temporal and then find the bridge by which to cross into the joy and peace of the eternal, He came down to Bethlehem as the Lamb of God to shed the atoning blood for the sins of all people. When the tensions between men reach their horrible climax in strife, bloodshed and tribulation, however, He will return as the Lion of the Tribe of Judah to finish the ultimate battle and act as the righteous judge of all people. Until the coming of that day, as we count each new year going forward from Bethlehem, "house of bread" and storehouse of abundant waters, Jesus Christ waits and offers to all people the bread of life and the living water.

"I am the bread of life; he who comes to me will not hunger, and he who believes in Me will never thirst.... Everyone who drinks of this water will thirst again; but whoever drinks of the water that I will give him shall never thirst; but the water that I will give him will become in him a well of water springing up to eternal life" (John 6:35 and 4:13-14).

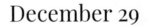

December 29

THE STAR AND THE JOY

*⁷ Then Herod secretly called the Magi and determined from them the exact
time the star appeared. ⁸ And he sent them to Bethlehem and said, "Go
and search carefully for the Child; and when you have found Him, report
to me, so that I too may come and worship Him." ⁹ After hearing the
king, they went their way; and the star, which they had seen in the east,
went on before them until it came and stood over the place where the Child
was. ¹⁰ When they saw the star, they rejoiced exceedingly with great joy.*

Matthew 2:7-10

As the triumvirate of paranoia, panic, and rage swelled
within Herod's troubled spirit, the king appears to have
kept it bottled up. Realizing that he could not afford to lift
a hand against the Magi and that it would be unwise even to
offend them, he puts up his best diplomatic front. If he could
not risk any quarrel with the Parthians to the east and would
have to wait to plead his case with Augustus in the west, he
could at least seize the moment to deal with the minor matter

of this ridiculous rumor of some newborn King of the Jews. In so doing, Herod would be taking an action not so much to protect his throne as simply to remind all in Palestine who truly was the king of the Jews and would remain so.

Herod had not survived so long ruling a volatile populace on a coveted strip of land between the two world superpowers by being stupid or without the capacity for charm. Thus he does not castigate the Magi for their strange question but empathizes with them. Rather than condemning their long quest under the light of some guiding star, he joins it, even to the point of inquiring as to when they had first noticed this strange star. Then, having serenely provided them with hospitality, food and drink in the typical manner of the East, he sends them south to Bethlehem with his blessing. "Go and search carefully for the Child; and when you have found Him report to me, so that I too may come and worship Him." That the Magi, to some degree, may have seen through the king's façade seems possible and even likely, but any such presumption is purely speculation. Nevertheless, a lesson that can be taken here by all is that of the manifold and multifaceted manifestations of the workings of iniquity. Evil will not always appear aggressively, may not appear or announce itself as an enemy, can often be attractively ensconced in a pleasant aura, and frequently presents itself as agreeable, accepting, and inclusive. Such strategies and tactics are as old as Eve's earliest encounter with the serpent.

Whatever their level of discernment may have been, the Magi did not much dwell upon it. Still keenly focused as they had been for months or perhaps more than a year, they left Jerusalem and rode south toward Bethlehem, apparently under the cover of darkness. For we are told that they again saw the light of the star. "The star, which they had seen in the east, went on before them until it came and stood over the place where the child was." So the star that had been put before them from the beginning had remained shining before them, drawing and guiding them to their journey's end. Just as intriguing as is the mystery of the star itself, however, is what is conveyed in the brief verse that follows. "When they saw the star, they rejoiced exceedingly with great joy."

For many, the word "joy" is among the first to come to mind upon arrival of the season of Advent and Christmas and for good reason. In addition to the general rise in gaiety and festivities concurrent with the season are the timeless words of the angel to the shepherds on the night of Jesus' birth. "Do not be afraid; for behold, I bring you good news of great joy which will be for all the people." Indeed, regardless of one's mood, situation, condition, status, or location, the coming down from heaven unto earth of a Savior for all people surely is cause for joy.

Joy, though, like love, may be a concept often not fully understood and, thus, a word sometimes misused. Joy, as defined in Merriam-Webster's Collegiate Dictionary, is "the emotion evoked by well-being, success, or good fortune or by the prospect of possessing what one desires: delight: the expression or exhibition of such emotion: gaiety: a state of happiness or felicity: bliss: a source or cause of delight." To be sure, all the above can accompany a state of joy and be revelatory of it, but is such a definition adequate? Is it complete?

The answer may depend upon the depth with which one chooses to define the words and phrases composing the definition. Furthermore, scholars do have to work within the limits of the small space allotted for each entry. That acknowledged, though, it seems fair to suggest that most would define or identify joy by the overt, visible manifestations of gaiety, mirth, and delight. Smiles, laughter, shouts of exuberance, and giddiness would be telling signs.

While such overt manifestations can indicate the presence of genuine joy flowing out from within a person, they can never be consistent or certain indicators. As Solomon observed in Ecclesiastes 7:3, "For when a face is sad a heart may be happy." Given this indisputable truth, the reverse then is also true. A face may appear happy when the heart is truly sad. Most, possessing a modicum of discernment, will have observed such opposites and ironies of outer appearance versus inner reality on multiple occasions. They are often readily apparent in our current culture. In bars, clubs, at parties, and New Year celebrations—to suggest but a few potential venues, one often can see individuals using alcohol, drugs, with incessant noise, empty but incessant chatter, and constant activity to try to compensate for the emptiness, sadness and/or loneliness being carried on the inside. Though most such social gatherings feature smiles, laughter, and outward manifestations of exuberance, all frequently belie the emptiness of genuine joy in spirit and heart.

Joy, while correctly classified as an emotion, is also possessed of a spiritual quality. Therein lies the key to the greatest joy. This is not to assert, as some have, that only Christians can possess genuine joy. To the contrary, seemingly most people, regardless of faith or belief, are capable of experiencing joy. As for the nature, depth, and sustaining of the joy, however, there may be marked differences.

Because joy holds within its composition a spiritual element and verifiably cannot be attained by material resources, the source of the greatest joy surely must be a spiritual one. "Every good thing given and every perfect gift is from above, coming down from the Father of lights" (Jms 1:17). The prophet wrote of the people, "They offered great sacrifices and rejoiced because God had given them great joy" (Neh 12:43). Isaiah wrote of the Lord's own, "And the ransomed of the Lord will return and come with joyful shouting to Zion, with everlasting joy upon their heads. They will find gladness and joy and sorrow and sighing will flee away" (Isa 35:10). David, in Psalm 16:11, wrote, "You will make known to me the path of life; in Your presence is fullness of joy; in Your right hand there are pleasures forever." Then in Psalm 51:12, at one of the darkest and lowest points of his life, "Restore to me the joy of Your salvation."

Every good thing, every perfect gift, everlasting joy and the fullness of joy forever all flow from one source. All are the gift of the sole living God made fully manifest in the grace upon grace poured out in the sending down of His only begotten Son. The ultimate joy, the fullness of joy, and the everlasting joy all come down interlaced in the joy of His salvation. The eternal fullness of joy everlasting can never be purchased or taken but only received from the nail-scarred hand of Jesus Christ our Lord.

"The star, which they had seen in the east, went on before them until it came and stood over the place where the child was. When they saw the star, they rejoiced exceedingly with great joy." What were the countenances, outer expressions, and exclamations of the Magi in their joy—we do not know. We are not told, but we do know the source of their fullness of joy. For the source of their joy and the source of their epiphany was one and the same. That source was the living God, who had made known to them the coming of a king unlike any the world had known and the establishment of a kingdom of a kind inconceivable to men up to that point. That the kingdom would have neither borders nor frontiers, and that all people as free citizens would be welcomed to share in its riches, glory, and peace surpassing all comprehension was the irrepressible catalyst of great joy. Indeed, "they rejoiced exceedingly with great joy." Exceedingly is an adverb defined as "to an extreme degree."

The epiphany that had been given them at the appearance of the strange star in the east, the promise of a universal king of heaven and earth, the continual appearance of the star's guiding light drawing them evermore westward and now to the south and, at last, the star coming to rest and casting its beam upon a small house as the little town slept. In it all they could only rejoice to an extreme degree. Extensive knowledge and a depth of wisdom notwithstanding, they still had not the answers to all questions or complete understanding of the ramifications for all people in what they were about to behold. Yet the fullness of joy filled their hearts and they rejoiced to an extreme degree.

While many efforts have been made by numerous writers and pundits to arrive at a natural explanation for the guiding star, the fact remains that likely we will never solve the mystery of its identity and the form of its appearance. Could it have been some natural phenomenon set in motion by the hand of God long before to be manifested at the Advent of His Son? Surely it could have been a star created and manifested by Him just at the time when He wished to draw the eyes of the Magi to the west in preparation for the epiphany they would receive. Noteworthy, though, is what appears to have happened as they drew up before the small house where their epiphany would be consummated.

Standing before a row of houses under a clear night sky, looking up, and then determining which star high above stands over which house is tricky. Pick one out of the many in your focused upward gaze (remembering that hundreds would have filled even a narrow probe of Bethlehem's sky then). Yet if you then step over to the next house and then the next, you will find your selected star appears to stand above them as well. In fact, drive over to another neighborhood and you will find your star standing over its houses as well.

This star, which drew the Magi from far in the east to Jerusalem and then to Bethlehem, did something that stars do not do. It "went on before them until it came and stood over the place where the child was." Thus it seems to have moved in an unnatural pattern and then to have identified the very house in which the Lord Jesus rested or perhaps a small group of houses for the Magi to figure out the rest. By what manner was this accomplished? A downward beam of light acting as a spotlight to illuminate the house? Rays of descending light like laser beams hitting the house? We can speculate and imagine, but we cannot know. Yet somehow, the star they had followed for so many miles went before them and shined down upon the house they were to enter.

They rejoiced exceedingly with great joy because a journey had been completed in which faith and months, or perhaps even years, of yearning, seeking, searching, and striving had been rewarded. A spiritual quest had been supernaturally fortified and guided. An epiphany given in the still silence of the realms of heart and mind was about to be manifested fully in flesh and blood before their own eyes. Under the light of the star that had brought them from afar they would look into the living eyes that were the "Light of men," the "Bright Morning Star."

December 30

WORSHIP: CONSUMMATION OF THE EPIPHANY

[11] After coming into the house they saw the Child with Mary His mother; and they fell to the ground and worshiped Him.

Matthew 2:11a

Despite much that has been speculated or asserted, the actions of the Magi in verse eleven make clear beyond shadow of doubt that their quest, in its entirety, was solely spiritual. Never had their journey been in any way concerned with the earthly affairs of men, rulers, or nations. What Herod the King could not fathom had, by the transcendence of God, been made understood to them. There would be a king in this world but not of this world, whose kingdom would be unlike any other ever known or imagined, and He would gather that kingdom from the people of every nation, tribe, and tongue even to the ends of the earth. Furthermore, that entrance into that kingdom was never to be determined by ethnicity, status, class, wealth, good works, or pious demeanor but, rather, only by the dispositions of heart and mind. This revelation had been their epiphany. So here, as they enter the house in Bethlehem and look upon eternity in the Christ Child's eyes, we see the culmination of the epiphany.

In America and much of the West, we have a culture in which it would seem that many adults regard children as intellectual and philosophical equals. Few would admit to such, but what we observe all around us suggests that it is so. With each passing week, parents can be seen negotiating with recalcitrant youth or tantrum-throwing children, as opposed to holding firm and trying their best to teach and enforce appropriate behavior. We see them placate temper fits and open defiance rather than drawing a line, staying on it, and striving to cultivate what is proper and good. Often, my wife and I have heard our peers complain about feeling they were merely the unpaid chauffeurs for their children for all their extracurricular activities. "But you have to let them do all these things," they explain resignedly. On a level more degenerate and disturbing, some appear to think, or have said outright, that their job as a parent is to be their child's friend. They wish to be a companion or a "buddy," not control the child's life or dictate his actions. A more distressing facet of this phenomenon may be observed in those parents who begin to behave like their youth and children as they attempt to "do life with them," or in mothers who begin to try to dress like their daughters or even their granddaughters!

Of these traits of modern Western culture there was absolutely no equivalent in the ancient East. There was nothing even to faintly resemble them. To fully comprehend and appreciate what happens here in verse eleven, this must be understood. Upon seeing the Child Jesus with Mary His mother, they fell to the ground and worshipped Him. These Magi, even being among the elite of their great empire, fell to the ground, bowed down, and worshipped a Child! Why? They worshipped the Child because they understood and believed in their hearts that this Child was unlike any other child born of woman before or that would be so born ever again. For no other reason would Magi have bowed in worship of a child. They bowed before the Child and worshipped because they saw that epiphany bestowed silently upon mind and heart made flesh before them. The divine promise inherent in the epiphany had been fulfilled as they looked upon the reward of their journey and the most profound possible blessing of the openness and obedience of their hearts.

Worship, for many around the world, is an important part of the season of Advent, Christmas, and Epiphany, and so it should be for all believers. Yet what did it truly mean, and what was fully entailed when the Magi fell and worshipped the Christ Child? For the sake of clarity and the definition of terms, we might ask, "What is worship?" Is there anything to be taken from the Magi's worship that might be relevant for believers today? What of other passages of Scripture addressing the subject? Is worship, in and of itself, a subject that needs to be reflected upon and contemplated in our postmodern era?

Let us begin with the last of the above questions. The answer is, unfortunately, verifiably and indisputably, "yes." All would do well to reflect upon and contemplate genuine worship, and to do so honestly and without preconceived notions. Many pastors in the evangelical denominations, if so inclined, could talk for hours about the incessant arguments, conflicts, and infighting they have witnessed and tried to mediate with regard to the issue of proper worship for lack of a better term. The choice of music, while not always the only issue, is generally at the forefront of such disputes.

Numerous pastors have told me, regarding the argument and bickering over selection of music and style of worship, that "it just never stops."

Nor are their accounts difficult to believe, for books and many articles have been written in recent years on the so-called "worship wars." The fact that such a term— "worship wars"—has even been coined is sufficient in itself to answer the question before us in the affirmative. The term, nevertheless, appears to have been well chosen, for in churches all across our nation, the indoor battlefields of the "worship wars" are awash with the sights, sounds, and carnage of this distinct brand of holy war. Furthermore, countless individuals over the years have told me, when explaining why they chose a certain church, that style of worship and music was their primary, and often their only, criterion in making said choice. Many others who had left a church or been a part of splitting a church gave as their paramount or sole reason for so doing exactly the same. Seminaries and colleges have classes and degree programs wholly devoted to church worship and church music. Therein, Christian academia attempts to light the path leading toward the heaven-endorsed truth of what precisely constitutes the proper mode of worship and accompanying style of music for today's churches and parachurch events. All that appears to be discernible for certain is that almost all involved have a very definite opinion.

In a recent conversation with several seminary professors, I mentioned an old Christmas carol of which I have been fond since childhood, "We Three Kings of Orient Are." A professor of church music just looked at me and shook his head in the negative. Upon my surprised inquiry, he explained, "You can't do that one in churches now. Nothing with minor keys. Those make people feel sad. You have to do songs that uplift them and make them feel happy." That was something I had not known, though perhaps there is much in the modern church that eludes my understanding.

Given that most have a definite opinion and few seem willing to give any ground, we might do well to continue back up through the previous questions. What does the Bible tell us about worship? The answer, on balance, is very little—less at least than many might presume.

There is absolutely no format of worship, or no order of worship or order of service given in Holy Scripture for the Church of our Lord Jesus Christ. None! This is important to understand because this must be the starting point for any wishing to contemplate the subject honestly and in full.

We are commanded to worship our Lord through song, in singing His praises as in Psalms 95, 96 and 100, and with various musical instruments as in Psalm 98. Examples of worship through song continue in the New Testament in Acts 16, Colossians 3 and in Hebrews 2. Then we are granted a glimpse into heavenly worship (see Revelation 5, 14, and 15), which incorporates song with both voice and instruments and appears to be powerful, energetic, moving, and quite loud at times. What we are not given is any mandated structure, formula, style, or specific lyric guidelines for songs of worship. Suffice it to note that the songs we sing in worship today sound nothing like the Hebrew psalms or the music of the first-century church. That such musical change was inevitable with the passing of centuries and the spread of the Gospel through the world to every nation, tribe, and tongue is revealing of at least one reason why no specific form or style of worship music was mandated in Scripture.

Extensive instructions for worship and ritual were given for the tabernacle in Exodus and Leviticus, and then for the temple in 1 and 2 Chronicles. While much of value might be taken therefrom, there also are obvious limitations to what can be taken with regard to the worship of the New Testament church. Moreover, beyond the instructions for the tabernacle and temple, there remains little regarding any formal structures in worship.

In 1 Corinthians 14, Paul gives instructions for an orderly worship, indicating that worship has order, clarity, and coherence. So worship must have order. What is neither commanded nor even offered is an order of worship. Put another way, no format or formal structure is offered. There is nothing that might resemble the order set forth in many church bulletins on Sundays in the postmodern West.

What is given clearly throughout Scripture are various elements of worship. The worship through song with instrument and voice has been noted. Further, we find emphasis upon teaching and preaching in Acts 2, 5, 8, and 14 and in 1 Corinthians 14. Prayer is instructed as a requisite of worship in numerous passages, including Acts 2, Matthew 6, Ephesians 6, and 1 Thessalonians 5. To worship with prayers of thanksgiving is commanded numerous times in both the Old and New Testaments. The reading aloud of Scripture is commanded in 1 Timothy 4 and Nehemiah 8. The ordinances of baptism and communion are to be central to church worship, as revealed in Matthew 28 and Acts 2, as well as in Luke 22 and 1 Corinthians 11 respectively.

While worship can be vigorous and loud, even with instruments and dancing (Ps 150), we also learn that worship can be still and silent. "Meditate in your heart upon your bed, and be still" (Psalm 4:4). Psalm 62:1, 5 and Isaiah 41:1 and Lamentations 3:26 speak of waiting upon the Lord and listening to Him in silence. Prayers can be uttered aloud or in silence. The Meditation upon the Word to which we are commanded must be a silent form of worship.

Moving back toward the question of "What is worship," Jesus Himself provided greater clarity to be taken along with the elements given. "But an hour is coming, and now is, when the true worshippers will worship the Father in spirit and truth; for such people the Father seeks to be

His worshippers. God is spirit, and those who worship Him must worship in spirit and truth" (John 4:23-24). The point Jesus makes here is that worship is no longer confined to a particular place (tabernacle or temple) and is not accomplished by ritual. Rather, it is to be based upon the spiritual relationship between the worshipper and the living God. Such a relationship is made possible only through faith in the sole mediator between God and man, our Lord Jesus Christ.

Thus while worship has physical manifestations and takes an outer form, genuine worship of the living God must be a function of spirit, heart, and mind. Of this there can be neither doubt nor debate. True worship wells within and flows from the human spirit as a product of the immortal soul, traveling through a spiritual conduit, and then is received spiritually by our God, who is spirit. If there is song, dance, exhortation, or prayer with neither a spiritual catalyst nor a spiritual connection, there can be no genuine worship. The preaching, praying, singing, or performing could be very good and even biblically sound. Yet if they have not a spiritual source within the one who speaks, sings, or performs, that one cannot be truly engaged in worship.

So what, then, in accordance with Scripture, is worship? Worship is a state of the spirit, heart, and mind. Worship may take on numerous outer manifestations. Words of gratitude or praise, the voice in song, the playing of musical instruments, exhortation, testimony, and the bearing of witness, the reading aloud of sacred Scripture, reflections upon His sacrifice and grace while taking the bread and wine, and the still silence of meditation upon His Word all are acts of worship that may flow from a spirit and heart being in a state of genuine worship.

All these same actions, of course, could come forth from the mouths and hands of those whose spirits and hearts do not hold the genuine state of worship. By our human definitions of action and word, all these things must still constitute forms of worship. If, however, we take to mind and heart all that can be discerned in Scripture, then any of the above actions manifested in one whose spirit and heart is not possessed of a genuine state of worship would not be received by our Lord as true worship. Remember Jesus' admonitions to the Pharisees about their vain repetitions and many words. His point was that even when their words and actions were right, their hearts were still far from Him. Worship may take many forms, be energetic or still, resounding or silent, liturgical or informal, but only that proceeding from spirits and hearts being in true states of worship can be received as worship by the living God.

So what, then, do we see in the Magi's worship of the Christ Child in Bethlehem? What do we take from it? The spirits and hearts of the Magi had been prepared for worship over hundreds of miles of riding as they followed their guiding star. In fact, their spiritual preparation began long before they took out their saddles and gathered equipment and supplies. The epiphany had been given to them, but to receive that epiphany, minds and hearts had to be open and spirits humble. What is there, then, we must ask, in a humble spirit with open mind and heart? There are the seeds of true worship planted in fertile ground, needing only the rain of Heaven to bring them to fruition.

In spirit, mind, and heart, then, the Magi were prepared for worship before their journey began. Yet worship entails therein another requisite component. That is obedience. The newborn King of Kings was not going to be brought to them. They had to go to Him, and to go to much effort and expense and take much time to do so. Counter to all worldly logic and wisdom, however, they obeyed unflinchingly the silent command inherent in their epiphany. With spirits humbled and hearts and minds open, they would travel as far as the star would lead them.

The spiritual preparation of the Magi is evident as they enter the house and first look upon the Child Jesus, for the worship and outward acts thereof commenced immediately. There are no precursors or intervening episodes in the text. "They saw the Child with Mary His mother; and they fell to the ground and worshipped Him."

When they looked into the Christ Child's eyes, the rain of heaven fell upon the fertile grounds and seed of humbled spirits and open hearts and minds. Then worship in its purest form sprang forth naturally and irrepressibly. Whether or not they spoke words to Him or over Him we cannot know, but actions always are far more revealing than words. In falling upon the ground before Him and bowing down to Him in humility and reverence, they gave to Him all honor, glory, gratitude, and praise, which together are the quintessence of true worship. There was no preacher, priest, exhorter, worship leader, praise band, choir, or orchestra. There was no testimony, prophesying, or singing. Nothing that we associate with the word "worship" in our church today was present there, and yet there was genuine worship. This we can know with certainty from what is revealed in the text.

Yes, even without the professionals and accoutrements often considered necessary for worship today, there was worship in its purest form in the little house in Bethlehem. The Magi had come with a spirit of worship, and in spirit and truth they worshipped the King of all Kings and Lord of all Lords. Their worship had an outward manifestation as, indeed, they fell upon the ground and bowed before Him, but their actual worship welled within.

Amid the many styles of worship and music, the numerous thoughts and strong opinions thereof, and even with the so-called "worship wars," there would seem much of significance to be taken by the modern church regarding the Magi's worship. Based upon Scripture, worship can never be defined as merely an event, a particular action, or a sequence of actions. Because true worship is not an outward act but an inner disposition, worship can be lifted up to God at any time, in any place, and in any circumstance. Genuine worship is in no way confined to the church grounds or dependent upon accoutrements or personage. When a state of worship is cultivated and maintained in spirit, heart, and mind, we can then worship freely, whether alone or in a group and regardless of surroundings and styles.

December 31

THE GIFTS

> *¹¹ Then, opening their treasures, they presented to Him gifts of gold, frankincense, and myrrh.*
>
> Matthew 2:11b

The giving of gifts and the receiving of gifts on Christmas day, especially for children, are anticipated and enjoyed traditions of our Christmas observance. In parts of Europe and Latin America, the primary day for the giving of gifts for children has traditionally been January 6, a custom of the observance of Epiphany that continues in many places today. Practices vary by country and culture, but one that is common is for the children to put out some grain for the camels of the Magi, hoping in return to receive gifts from the kindly wise men. When the children arise on Epiphany morn, they find the camels have eaten their fill and presents await them in their shoes or in the box or trough that had held the grain the night before. The custom of giving gifts on Epiphany is quite logical, for it seems clear that our giving of gifts on Christmas stems primarily from the gifts brought by the Magi on the first Christmas. In our observance and keeping of the spirit of both days, my wife and I long have exchanged gifts on Christmas and Epiphany, remembering the ultimate gift to all people is Emmanuel, Jesus our Savior, and then remembering the true joy to be found in giving to those we cherish and love.

While there is no Scriptural mandate for the giving of gifts at Christmastime, for those having the resources to give, to do so would seem to be within the spirit both of the season and of the Way of Christ in general. The one thing the follower of Christ should not do, though, is allow the gift-giving or any other facet of the holiday festivities to overshadow the true reason for our remembrances and the purposes to be accomplished through our observances and reflections or the reason for the season. In any given December, one can see the pendulum swinging to either extreme. There are those whose focus is solely upon the festivities, the parties, and the material facets of the holidays. On the other hand, I have often encountered those who claim to hate the gift-giving aspect of Christmas, dreading toward the end of every Fall what they see as the coming unavoidable obligation to find and purchase the right gift for all. The ultimate emptiness and spiritual bankruptcy in the former are readily apparent. As for the latter, perhaps they should exclude themselves from the annual gift exchange until they can discover the blessing and the joy that can be attained through giving.

The joy felt by the Magi as they opened their treasures before the Christ Child is palpable in verse eleven. The joy in their presentation of the gold, frankincense, and myrrh was a heightened extension of the joy that had welled within them when the star had settled and shined down upon the little house in Bethlehem. Having then looked into the eyes of the newborn King of Kings, the fullness of joy and an overflowing of blessings came with the opportunity to lay before Him their finest gifts.

The gifts had a material value and a soon-to-be-realized temporal purpose. First and foremost, however, the gifts were spiritual. In the spiritual symbolism of the gifts is further revealed the depth and specific nature of the epiphany the Magi had received.

Gold is the precious metal valued above all others and against which virtually all other mediums of exchange are measured. Thus gold is seen as symbolic of kingship, an abundant possession of kings, the gift of kings, and the appropriate gift for a king. The Magi presented gold as a symbol of the coming of the King of all Kings whom they understood was to be like none other, as the two other gifts will reveal. That they chose to present gold to a child king who, as of yet, had been recognized by no other person or nation as King is in and of itself revealing of their understanding of the spiritual nature of this King and His Kingdom.

Gold was abundant in numerous regions of Asia, and Ethiopia was also often a source of gold in the ancient Near East. Ancient Arabia held an abundance of a particularly striking form of gold often referred to as "red" gold or "fireless" gold. Diodorus wrote of the Arabian gold, praising its beauty and purity, in the first century B.C. He noted the gold's fiery-red hue and explained the designation of "fireless" by the fact that the Arabian red gold was not smelted from ore but was taken from the earth in chestnut-sized nuggets. The gold of Arabia (Sheba) is mentioned by Solomon in Psalm 72:15, where he prophesies that it will be given to the King to whom all kings will bow down and all nations will serve and who will deliver the poor and needy and the afflicted and will have compassion on them. Further, the king who receives the Arabian gold will "rule from sea to sea and from the River to the ends of the earth." His name will endure forever, will increase as long as the sun shines, and men will bless themselves by him. More than nine hundred years before the Magi rode into Bethlehem, it would appear that King Solomon experienced a similar epiphany.

While we cannot know the source of the gold brought by the Magi, we do know that they brought it for a king and gave it as a symbol of His kingship. This was appropriate and telling, for it was the kingship of the Christ Child that was to be the stumbling rock set before all people. Upon that rock all would ultimately either stumble and fall or rise with His kingship as the precious cornerstone of their royal, eternal priesthood.

As Charles E. Jefferson observed, the world has long been willing, even eager, to accept Jesus Christ as gentle teacher, ethical guide, noble philosopher, poet, righteous reformer, or lover of humanity. They hesitate, however, only when asked to acknowledge and serve Him as king. Yet upon His assertion of being the eternal King, He was neither relenting nor flexible. When Pilate asked Him if He was the King, Jesus replied, "It is as you say." As King, moreover, He never wavered in His insistence upon absolute obedience and loyalty from all people. Again, here people and nations stumble. Many and likely most can readily accept the wise teacher, the noble philosopher, or the great advocate of universal love; but in light of His claim as King, the true thoughts and intentions of every heart are revealed (Luke 2:35; Heb 4:12). Before His commands of absolute loyalty and obedience, human adherence, affections, and superlatives quickly fade. Rejection then holds consistent and firm; and, as when He stood before Pilate in the beginning, outright hostility so often has followed as it still does today.

Yet the incomparable blessing and sublime beauty in the kingship of the wholly righteous King of Kings may fail to be realized. The bringing of ultimate justice, the establishment of eternal peace, and the prevailing of true righteousness all hinge upon the emergence and action of an omnipotent and truly righteous king. Any who believe that humans and their governments and countless organizations are going to solve the world's problems, establish genuine justice for all, usher in permanent peace, or set mankind on a perpetual path to righteousness have understood surprisingly little of the annals of human history or of the tides of our postmodern world rising all around them. Only in the coming and action of a king of righteousness greater than all other kings and nations and more powerful than the spiritual forces of evil can justice be upheld, lasting peace secured, and righteousness vindicated and ascendant forevermore. All these things, as He repeatedly made clear, He will accomplish in His time in accordance with the will and plan of His Father.

The beauty and the blessing in the meantime, as His plan unfolds and the time draws near, is in that which the King of Righteousness offers to all who accept His kingship in obedience. First there is His unconditional and sacrificial love for each one of us. And what earthly king ever has given the admonitions to love as his first two commands? To love your God and love all people, loving each other in the same way that He loved us. Second, there is the inner, spiritual peace which surpasses all comprehension. No man, government, organization, corporation, or human endeavor can be the giver of such a peace. Third, there is life abundantly and life eternal. The joy, peace, contentment, purpose, and comfort amid life's storms in aggregate are a gift that He only can give. Then the doors into life eternal in His heavenly kingdom, opened by the atonement in His blood and His triumph o'er the grave, through which all who serve Him as King will enter.

That a king, omnipotent and ever righteous, was coming was understood to the Magi in their epiphany. That such a king, for the sake of mankind, had to come, while also being inherent in the epiphany, would have been understood to them from their keen observations of life, the cosmos, history, and nations. For they were men wise to the ways of the world, the ways of people and the ways of nature. That their journey following the star would take them to the eternal and wholly righteous King of Kings, they understood. Thus the gift of gold, signifying the King had come and declaring before Him and all men their submission to His rule.

Frankincense is a resinous substance taken from certain trees in the balsam family. The primary source of frankincense has always been the Arabian peninsula, particularly the southern regions where the trees grow in abundance. The horn of Africa (modern-day Somalia) also has long produced an abundance of frankincense.

The Greek historian Herodotus wrote in the fifth century B.C. of Arabia's tremendous wealth in spices, naming frankincense, myrrh, cassia, cinnamon, and gum-mastich. Pliny the Elder, in the first century A.D., also wrote specifically of Arabian frankincense and myrrh. Identifying a people known as the Sabaeans in the district of Sabaei, he notes as the backbone of their economy the production, export, and trade of frankincense and myrrh, and also claims them as the originators of that trade. Sabaei, or Saba, is the biblical Sheba, from whence came the wealthy and powerful queen whose visit to Solomon's court is recorded in 1 Kings 10. Verse ten notes a large amount of spices as being among the gifts she brought to Solomon, so great that, "Never again did such an abundance of spices come in as that which the Queen of Sheba gave King Solomon." Chief among these spices, of course, would have been frankincense and myrrh. Diodorus, in the first century B.C., asserted that it had been frankincense and myrrh that made the kingdom of Sheba the wealthiest in the ancient world.

By the time the Magi received their epiphany, trade routes for frankincense and myrrh, as well as for other spices, were extensive and had long been established. While the Sabaeans and others in southern Arabia likely controlled the trade for millennia, by the time of Christ's birth, control had shifted north to the Nabataeans, the Arab builders of the famed ancient city of Petra. Desired by so many and so lucrative was this trade that whoever had the power to control product, roads, and trade would always do so.

Frankincense was used throughout the ancient world in perfumes, scented oils, and as a fragrant incense. In Hebrew culture, religion and Mosaic law, frankincense had significance deeper than its aesthetic value. Pure frankincense was commanded by the Lord to Moses in Exodus 30:34 as one of the spices to be used exclusively in the incense to be burned in the Tabernacle. The fragrant, rising smoke of the incense was to be symbolic of the prayers of God's people being lifted up to Him. Thus in Luke 1, as the multitude stood outside in prayer, the priest Zacharias entered the temple and burned incense on the altar of incense. Further, we see in John's vision in the heavenly scene of Revelation 8 a pause in the terrible judgments of the great tribulation period as an angel added much incense to the prayers of the saints and placed it on the coals of the golden altar before the throne of almighty God. Even amid the terrors and wrath of His judgment, the living God hears and considers the prayers of His people. Like the wafting smoke of frankincense to human scent, the rising prayers of His own are always sweet and pleasing to our Lord.

As spiritual shepherds of the people and as their intercessors before God lifting up prayers to Him on their behalf, priests were indelibly linked with the burning of frankincense. For frankincense was symbolic of their role of intercessor and mediator between God and men prior to the emergence of the one who was to become the sole Mediator and High Priest for all people. David said of Him in Psalm 110—the one whom he called "my Lord," sitting at the right hand of "the Lord" — "You are a priest forever according to the order of Melchizedek." Melchizedek who, according to Hebrews 7, is the King of Righteousness and Peace and who is without father, mother, and genealogy, having neither beginning of days nor end of life and, like the Son of God, remains a priest perpetually. What is clearly suggested here is that He whom David called, "my Lord," and Melchizedek are one and the same, our Lord Jesus Christ, the perpetual priest and priest forever.

To the priest forever for all people the Magi brought frankincense, the symbol of His eternal priesthood and of their own acknowledgement of Him as the sole priest between themselves and the living God forevermore. By their own statement to Herod, we can know that they came seeking a king. Thus gold could be said to have been a logical gift. Apart from a very specific revelation given them in their epiphany, however, they are unlikely to have considered frankincense, a product not even native to their homeland. Yet the epiphany had revealed to them not only a king like none other but also the perpetual priest for all people whose priesthood was from long ago and from the days of everlasting unto everlasting.

The necessity of the third gift, then, we can imagine must have been unsettling to the Magi—troubling and perhaps even confusing. For in their epiphany the birth of the eternal king and perpetual priest had been revealed to them, and yet the gift foretelling of great sacrifice and the preparation for death was also included.

Suppose that I was invited to a baby shower or to a child's first birthday party. As the other guests presented their gifts of baby clothes, cute stuffed animals, and breakproof infant tableware, I present to the new mother a beautifully packaged bottle of embalming fluid or an attractively wrapped baby coffin. Suffice it to say that, aside from the shock and disbelief of all present at my breach of etiquette, I would likely no longer be a welcome guest. Yet this, in essence, is what transpired when the Magi bowed down and presented the gift of myrrh.

While the precious aromatic resin had various uses in the ancient Near East—perfume and scented oils (Esth 2:12), anointing oil (Ex 30:23), and for scenting clothing as we do with cedar today (Ps 45:8) —myrrh was known by all for its use in treating and embalming the bodies of the dead. Given the inherent frequency of death, such was likely the most common use of myrrh in ancient times. We see an example of this in John 19:39 after Jesus' death when Nicodemus brought almost a hundred pounds of a myrrh and aloes mixture with which to treat His body before it was wrapped and entombed by Joseph of Arimathea.

In the gift of myrrh, even more than in the gold and frankincense, the clarity and depth of the epiphany given the Magi is revealed. For had the necessity and surety of sacrificial death not been clearly revealed to them, they would never have brought before a young mother, father, and child the gift of myrrh. Yet not only had the coming sacrifice been revealed to them. So, too, had they been given understanding of the nature of and reason for that sacrifice, and even that the resulting death of the sacrifice somehow, would not yield a permanent condition. For the myrrh of the ultimate sacrifice must be considered alongside the gold of the eternal king and the frankincense of the perpetual priest.

Was there some confusion or question in the minds of the Magi as to exactly how all this was to transpire? Were there questions as to the reasons why such was to be the way? Though we cannot know for certain, it would seem reasonable to suggest that some questions may have lingered.

Uncertainties notwithstanding, as to the nature and function of king, priest, and sacrifice, the Magi held clear understanding and calm assurance. A king who would open His kingdom to people of every nation, tribe, and tongue and who ultimately would usher in the eternal reign of true righteousness, justice, and peace. A perpetual priest who forever would be the conduit through which all people could reach their God, fellowship with Him, and receive His grace upon grace in the salvation of life eternal. A sacrifice that would be the atonement for all people, making possible salvation for all choosing to claim the saving power in His innocent blood and walk in His Way.

As learned men of the world, the Magi would have understood the concept of blood atonement, which pervades religion and culture the world over. What they saw in their epiphany and acknowledged with their gift of myrrh, however, was something unprecedented. The sacrifice and spilled blood of one wholly righteous and blameless was to be the atoning sacrifice before God for all people and for all time. The blood of no other creature or human need ever be shed. The iniquities of all people who accept and follow Him would be washed away in the flow of His precious blood, leaving them renewed, pure, and wholly acceptable before the living God.

We celebrate the King of Kings, the priest forever and the atoning sacrifice for all people. Let us also reflect upon the blessing of a righteous king, omnipotent and unbound by time, who accepts into His eternal Kingdom those of every nation, tribe, and tongue who call upon His name. Consider the blessedness of a perpetual priest who alone bridged the gulf between God and men, who forevermore removed the need of any other intermediary so that all people can approach their God alone, just as they are. Then reflect upon the sacrifice in which He in whom there was no deceit or sin Himself became deceit and every form of sin on behalf of all people as he bled out from the cross. Contemplate the fierceness and depth of the love that took Him to that cross and made Him pray for the forgiveness of those who cursed, mocked, beat, and killed Him. Finally, having examined the gifts of the Magi, let us consider the gifts we will lay before Him.

OUR OWN GOLD, FRANKINCENSE AND MYRRH

15 "If you love Me, you will keep My commandments.
John 14:15

Having reflected upon the gifts of the Magi as we begin a new year, the time is right to consider the gifts you will lay before the King of Kings. What will be your own gold, frankincense, and myrrh? While apparent enough that your modern gifts will not be literal gold, frankincense, and myrrh, you might do well to be cautious with presumption. A friend who pastored a church in Alaska some years back told me of regularly finding gold nuggets and bags of gold dust in the church's offering plate on Sunday mornings. Where the gold was coming from was never made known, but the pastor did learn the identity of the givers. Two faithful church members who lived far from town and eked out their living in the harsh Alaskan wild country knew where to find the gold; and having little actual money and few, if any, assets they gave the gold as their tithe.

So wise men do still set gold before their Lord on occasion. Moreover, those who support both the church and people in need with their own financial resources can be said to be doing the same. In a country blessed with the economic prosperity and resources that we enjoy in America, most can afford to give at least something, even if in small amounts, to support the church and those in need. With monetary giving excepted, though, the gifts that most of us bring before the King will, nevertheless, be quite different than the gold, frankincense, and myrrh of the Magi. We must ask, then, what should these gifts be?

Many have considered the answer to be simple. We should give all to Him, all that we are and all that we have. While there is an element of truth in this assertion, we also must be wary of carelessness with words. That everything we are and everything we have belongs to God and should be recognized as belonging to Him is true. For He is the giver of all life and of every blessing, gift, resource, and ability. This fact should never be taken lightly or for granted.

Where such a blanket assertion falls short is in the failure to recognize the simple, age-old realities of a life lived. Thus it then fails in the realms of requisite specificity and the defining of terms. A businessman must turn a profit and continually invest in his business. Otherwise he soon would have no business, no way to support his family, and no resources with which to help anyone else. A company employee must put in his hours at work and pay mortgages, car payments, and other bills. Without a home, job, and transportation, he could not support family or church or help anyone else. Though specific personal needs can vary by city, state, or nation, that such are always present and must be met remains a longstanding fact of life. In addressing the question of our gifts, however, there is no reason to speak with either vagueness or ignorance, for Scripture is quite clear on the matter.

We begin with Jesus' words to His disciples in John 14:15. "If you love Me, you will keep My commandments." The vast majority of Christians would claim to love their Lord Jesus Christ, and this they should do. For He made clear, in Matthew 22:36-40, that to love our God and then to love each other are the two foremost commands of the Law. Yet to say that we love our God or that we love anyone else is a simple thing. Mere statements or professions of love, as is made evident around us every day in all kinds of relationships, neither establish nor verify anything. To say that we love, and even to feel strongly that we love, comes quite naturally in many cultures. Jesus, however, always defined His terms in matters of vital import. Furthermore, He emphasized actions and the true state of the heart, from which actions ultimately flow, over any words spoken.

An example of this is the conversation between Jesus and Peter as related in John 21. While repeatedly inquiring as to the truth and degree of Peter's love for Him, Jesus seems to virtually ignore the claim inherent in Peter's words with every answer. Each time Peter affirmed his love, Jesus responded, not with approval or commendation, but with a stern command: "Tend My lambs, Shepherd My sheep," and "Tend My sheep." Jesus, in essence, says, "Don't tell Me how much you love Me, and don't tell others. Rather, go out and show Me through obedience and action that you truly love Me."

What Jesus said to Peter, He says to all of us who profess to love and follow Him. "If you love Me, you will keep My commandments." The gold, frankincense, and myrrh that all of us, regardless of situation and resources, can set before our Lord is that of an obedient life. Not a life perfect in obedience; for our Lord, knowing that imperfect humans are not capable of such, never demanded that. What He does command, in John 14:15 and elsewhere, is that we be perfect in our efforts to live an obedient life. The greatest gift we can give to Him, and the gift that will verify our professed love for Him, is to strive with all that is within us and with all that we have to live an obedient life. Such is greater in the eyes of our Lord than any amount of treasure or gold, than any eloquent sermon, than any amount of praise and worship, and than any achievement of individuals, churches, or organizations.

Within the essential gift of an obedient life set before our Lord, much is entailed. Much upon the path of obedience to our Lord is the same for all people. When considering specifically the gifts we are to bring, however, there will be great variance among individuals. This is acceptable, perfectly logical, and is fortunate. For our Lord, in His beauty and genius, created individuals, endowing each person with a distinct combination of capability, talent, inclination, and capacity of understanding and action. God designed us this way for an obvious reason. To meet the many and diverse challenges of life, making living as comfortable, productive, and secure as is possible, a tremendous diversity of inclinations, abilities, skills and knowledge is requisite.

I have not the knowledge or desire to work the farm fields and produce crops, but when I go to the grocery store, I am glad that other people do. Most people have no desire to probe around in the mouths of strangers; but when they need a dentist, they are glad that someone does. I have no ability for music but, loving music, am glad that others do. Many have not the capacity or inclination for constant, meticulous study and experimentation, but considering their reliance on technology in almost all facets of modern life; they can be glad others do. Obviously, such a listing could go indefinitely. The point to be understood is that God gave us all different gifts and inclinations for a reason. All are needed in the ongoing journey of life. No gift, talent, inclination, or combination thereof is superior or inferior to others. All simply constitute the gifts of God to and within each individual. The important question to be asked is not that of what your gifts are. Rather, the question as it relates to living an obedient life should be, "What do you do with his gifts?"

Peter, in 1 Peter 4:9, writes, "As each one has received a special gift, employ it in serving one another as good stewards of the manifold grace of God." So, as good stewards of the many blessings and abundant grace that God has bestowed upon each of us, we are then to use our gifts to serve and help others in the love and ways embodied by Jesus Christ. Whatever our gifts may be and whether great or seemingly limited by human ways of thinking, we should be willing to employ them for the sake of serving others.

This does not mean that our gifts cannot be utilized to help us make a living. Very often they will be or must be so used. An inclination toward deep study and a possession of natural oratory skills may allow a man to make his living as a pastor. This is fine, but regardless of his level of success or renown, he must remain cognizant of the first and primary duties of his calling, which is to be a faithful servant and shepherd to his people.

Most believers, though, are not employed in conventional ministry. Yet they can be effective ministers of Christ just as much as can any pastor. In fact, in many cases they might have a more extensive reach in their ministry than can a pastor or missionary. Always there are many unbelievers who, for a variety of reasons, are never going to darken the doors of any church but might be willing to listen to the gospel of Christ from one outside the church or from one who is respected for his work and accomplishments in some secular field.

Several of my friends, for example, are accomplished and highly respected in the field of archaeology and have been published by some of the most prestigious publishers. Their work, being purely based in science and historical documentation, is in a secular arena in which relatively few Christians are engaged. Yet because of their professionalism, skill, and accomplishment, they have had the opportunity to share the gospel of Christ with many highly educated men and women in their field who never would have received such a message in church or from pastor or priest. Further, these men have voluntarily used their understanding of science and history to help many in churches and colleges to better understand what they read in their Bibles.

I have seen this same type of situation play out in the very same way with successful people in multiple and greatly varied professions. Professional athletes, musicians, hunters, soldiers, police officers, doctors, nurses, physicists, coaches, cowboys, undertakers, IT personnel, and business people of almost every kind are among those who have employed their special gift to make a living but then also used that gift, and/or the renown and profits therefrom, to support the mission of the church. Note that not all the above occupations employ people who have wealth and/or fame. Each special gift within every person, regardless of how much or how little esteem is given them by the world, can be utilized to serve and to help others. In so doing we honor our Lord and, as Peter wrote, show ourselves to be "good stewards of the manifold grace of God."

The apostle Paul, in his second letter to the church in Corinth, also urged believers to be generous with their gifts and resources in reaching out to those in need. As we might expect with Paul, his instruction is more exhaustive than that of Peter. In 2 Corinthians 8, he extols the generosity of the Macedonian churches of which he notes, "that in a great ordeal of affliction their abundance of joy and their deep poverty overflowed in the wealth of their liberality. For I testify that according to their ability, and beyond their ability, they gave of their own accord." Then in verse 12, he adds this guideline to the mandate of giving of your special gifts and resources: "For if the readiness is present, it is acceptable according to what a person has, not according to what he does not have." Here Paul echoes the words of Jesus in Luke 12:48. "From everyone who has been given much, much will be required; and to whom they entrusted much, of him they will ask all the more." So our own gold, frankincense, and myrrh as presented to our Lord are to be determined by those special gifts He has given to each of us. Whether we give of our resources, unique abilities, or of both, we should do so in accordance with the degree we have been blessed by the generosity and grace of our Creator.

Though the Macedonian churches were commended for giving generously to a degree that appeared to be even beyond their limited capacities, note that none are asked to give beyond their means. What we give for the sake of Christ to serve and help others, rather, is "acceptable according to what a person has, not according to what he does not have." Those having little are asked to give only as they are able. One of the most profound testimonies to the unfathomable power of the gospel of Christ for the sake of goodness and lovingkindness is regularly made manifest in the number of devoted believers the world over who, like the Macedonian churches, so commonly give generously of all they have in measure significantly disproportionate to their meager resources. Nevertheless, our Lord is just and never asks more of us than we are able to accomplish.

For those who have been given much, though, much surely is required. None, no matter how intelligent, capable, wealthy, or powerful, prosper apart from the blessing and allowance of our Lord. Thus all who have been given much should count it a blessed privilege to give back generously of the portion they have been given. For as Paul continues on the matter in 2 Corinthians 9:7, "Each one must do just as he has purposed in his heart, not grudgingly or under compulsion, for God loves a cheerful giver." To give gifts that help others who cannot help themselves, be those gifts temporal or spiritual, is, as many have discovered, begetting of the greatest joy and satisfaction one can experience in this life apart from that of receiving the gift of our Lord's salvation.

We must never make light of the so-called temporal or material gifts. Not to presume, for example, that the work of one in the pastorate is more significant or important than what others may contribute with their special skills, abilities, or monetary resources. For in the world all around us are many diverse needs, challenges and problems, and very different skill sets, abilities, and capacities are required in the great endeavor to assist in as many such situations as possible. All special gifts given of God to each person are significant and are given for a reason. Every gift of every kind given in the Way of Christ by each individual according to what he has, therefore, also is of greatest significance.

While the ultimate immortality for all people is to be found only in receiving the gift that is the salvation of life eternal with our Lord Jesus Christ in His heavenly kingdom, there remains an earthly immortality to be gained. That immortality, however, is not one to be found, as a fountain of youth, or to be acquired as through diligent research or esoteric knowledge. Rather, it is an immortality to be attained by what we give.

When we make known the path of our Lord's salvation to another who accepts that gift, we have given a gift that not only will live beyond our earthly years but also that will live and resonate through eternity. Yet consider the matter further. If we give of time, ability, or resources, even gifts that are temporal and material and by so doing lift up one who had fallen and could not rise, or if we take from a path of personal destruction one whose life and hope of salvation soon would have been ended, then our earthly sojourn becomes immortal for having given an immortal gift. For such gifts so given touch not only the receiver of the gift but also his loved ones and family. As I have seen transpire numerous times, the receiver of the gifts, being lifted up or taken from the path of certain destruction, may go on to establish and raise a family who otherwise never would have been. Then each individual descended from the original receiver establishes a family, and so it continues unto eternity. This is the immortal gift through which earthly immortality is attained, then to be woven seamlessly into the ultimate immortality of life eternal with our Lord.

Should some reflect and yet still feel they have nothing worthy to give, consider the thoughts of Matthew Henry put to paper more than three hundred years ago. For any presuming they had nothing worthy to offer the King of Kings, he proposed a single question. Have you not a heart, even if dark and hard and unworthy of Him? Then give it to Him just as it is to use as it pleases Him. He will take the heart as it is, fill it, change it, and make it something better.

Begin by giving to Him your heart in full. He will make it His own, and with heart and spirit renewed, the vision of the spirit is established and the entirety of the field before you will come into focus. Then and there will begin to be made manifest the needs, challenges, emptiness, and pain of this world, and also the channels through which your own special gifts will flow out unto all who will receive them.

Being true to the Way of our Lord with the onset of a new year, we all should reflect upon what we will give. Echoing again the teaching of Jesus, Paul summarizes the matter of giving in 2 Corinthians 9:6: "Now this I say, he who sows sparingly will also reap sparingly, and he who sows bountifully will also reap bountifully." Whatever is to be our own gold, frankincense, and myrrh, let us count our blessings and then give with generosity and joy according to what He has given us.

WISE MEN SEEK HIM

¹³ You will seek Me and find Me when you search for Me with all your heart.
Jeremiah 29:13

Wise men still seek Him. We see the declaration on signs, ornaments, and cards throughout the Christmas season, often paired with an artistic rendering of three Magi astride their camels. If we can look beyond the fact that this slogan may have become a cliché within the backdrop of all human endeavor, history, the entirety of the earth, and the cosmos, then we begin to probe below the surface to the depths inherent in the fullness of these simple words and find a profound and timeless truth beginning to take form. Wise men do seek Him and the wise always will seek Him. The truly wise among men, regardless of where they were or how little had been revealed to them, always have sought Him.

Socrates sought Him. Plato sought Him. Aristotle sought Him. They sought truth in all things, but inherent in such a search is the ultimate quest for the Creator or, as Aristotle put it, the "unmoved mover."

The great, though little known, Chinese philosopher Mozi (470–391 B.C.)—sometimes written MoTzu—sought Him. In so doing, most remarkably, Mozi came closer to the gospel of Christ than did any pre-Christian philosopher or religious leader not accounted for in Scripture, including Plato. In fact, if we allow for the omission of the name of Jesus and His atoning action, as Mozi obviously had no way of knowing about Him or the living God of Israel, we can see that what Mozi taught was, in essence, the gospel that Jesus Christ was to embody and proclaim.

Others in diverse places and times also sought. While some of their names are known, surely those of many others are not known. Yet in any time and place, the unwise outnumber the wise. Those lacking the will and often even the desire to seek are to be more commonly found than the quiet, diligent seeker.

Some would dispute the veracity of the maxim. Many today, in fact, would say that to seek for a Creator and God is the antithesis of wisdom and that science has proven that there was no Creator while history shows that God is only a varied figment of the imaginations of men. Thus it would be fair to ask why the author and many others hold that the maxim is justified and profoundly true.

To begin, one cannot observe and contemplate objectively the natural world around us and not realize the presence and fingerprints of unfathomable genius, supreme power, and an irresistible force. The beauty, majesty, power and magnitude within our world and as deeply into the cosmos as we can see declare this presence. Too, all within declares design, which is why college students now in biology and other areas of science are often reminded by the writers of their texts that, though what they are seeing appears to be design, it is surely not design. Rather, all is but chance and mere coincidence.

The presence of water—to this point not found on any other planet and unexplained by scientists—alone reveals design and plan. For life cannot be sustained without it. The rivers, the seas, the rains, and the snows that sustain life are unique to earth. The rotation, revolutions, speed, and distances (such as between earth and the sun) all are perfect, just as they must be for life to go on.

Consider the power in just one volcano, one tornado, or one hurricane, realizing that each is but a fraction of all the power at work in the universe. Reflect then upon the fact that such can only be a mere infinitesimal of a fraction of the power held by the "unmoved mover" who designed all and put all into motion. Consider the power of an elephant, the blinding speed of a cheetah, the prowess and lethality of a lion, or the endurance of a camel and realize again the preeminence of the maker. The majesty of Mount Kilimanjaro on the Serengeti, the splendor of cactus flowers in bloom on the Sonoran Desert—fragile beauty amid unforgiving harshness—and the magnificence of the spectrum of color as sunset gives way to night on the desert all declare to us a majesty, splendor, and magnificence of a higher power for which our languages lack adequate words and our imaginations lack encompassment.

If we were only to observe and consider one thing, that being the cycle from conception to birth in humans—let alone the stimulations and driving forces that lead thereto—we are left again with the realization of a power and creative genius of design unapproachable and immeasurable to the collective human genius of the millennia. For the many who claim never to have witnessed a miracle, know that in the cycle of conception to birth we witness nothing less with each manifestation. For human beings, exposure to anything, however beautiful and resplendently revealing, so often leads to its being taken for granted. We might be tempted to invoke the old cliché: familiarity breeds contempt. Those truly wise will be wary of the danger of familiarity.

This indisputable evidence of a Creator in life itself and in all that we observe in the earth and cosmos is what Paul brings into play in the first chapter of his letter to the Romans. "That which is known about God is evident within them, for God made it evident to them. For since the creation of the world His invisible attributes, His eternal power and divine nature, have been clearly seen, being understood through what has been made, so that they are without excuse." This is not to imply that all who look upon the created order can know from it the redemptive work of Christ or the fine points of theology if such have never come before their eyes or been proclaimed to them. What is unequivocally asserted, though, is that all, regardless of knowledge, place, and time, looking first from within and then outward to all that surrounds them can and will understand that there is an "unmoved mover"—a creator—who can only be the living, divine, and omnipotent God of the universe. David was on a similar line of reflection when, a thousand years before Paul, he penned the opening words of Psalm 14. "The fool has said in his heart, 'There is no God.'"

Strong words, to be sure, but are they justified? Or do some people, understandably, just think and perceive things differently? To seek a just and verifiable answer, let us pull back from the earth and cosmos and look into the human mindset and process of deduction. Upon coming to a table and seeing a beautiful platter of artistically cut and arranged sushi, all would agree that somewhere there was a sushi chef. On being presented a fine, ornate katana, none would deny the presence and hands of a bladesmith and sword polisher. When entering a spectacular house, all would presume that there was an architect and builder. So it is for every single thing made, manufactured, or prepared in our world. Only when presented with something far greater, exceedingly more complex, and with a matchless collective splendor—the universe, our earth, and every living thing therein—do many then say, "There was no maker." Every object, mechanism, or concoction in their world they attribute to a maker, but for that which is the most diverse, majestic, beautiful, and imbued with the order and elements that sustain all life, they proclaim, "There is no creator. Something came from nothing and all came by chance."

First and foremost, the problem herein is one of logic and reason. For everything in their lives, they utilize one line of logic and one method of reason. Then, to account for and explain the biggest and most significant thing in all our lives, that same line of logic and method of reason is wholly abandoned for another. Such a thought process is severely inconsistent and is ultimately devoid of logic and reason. Furthermore, it is a process of thought that lacks intellectual honesty with yourself and with others. Intellectual honesty demands consistency of logic and reason. For a system of reason to be proven effective, let alone superior, it must be proven applicable in all situations. Genuine intellectual honesty, like logic and reason, inherently must be consistent. To shift to different methods when it becomes clear that using the established one cannot yield an answer acceptable to the seeker is not to expand thought, logic, or reason but to jettison them altogether.

"'Come now, and let us reason together,' says the Lord." The imploring words of Isaiah 1:18 remind us that our Creator is a God of reason. Reason, therefore, will guide you toward Him just the same as will the love of justice and righteousness.

Often it has been noted that many intelligent and learned people deny the existence of a creator and even the possibility of the existence of God. This is true, but two points should be understood. First, scientists with the acclaim given them in our society are only ever wrong in retrospect. Yet in retrospect they have been proven to be wrong many times. Second, the subject of this chapter is wisdom, not intellect or learning. While intelligence, learning, and wisdom can be present in the same individual and though all people, in accordance with Scripture, should strive to grow in knowledge and wisdom with each passing day, the fact is that there are many who are highly intelligent and hold vast knowledge but are lacking in wisdom. Conversely, there are some holding little knowledge and perhaps with limited capacities of intellect who yet possess profound wisdom. So though wisdom and knowledge often are linked, they are, in fact, two separate and distinct virtues. While to pursue and grow in both is the ideal, if one could only possess one or the other, wisdom is paramount. For it is by wisdom that we best discern the way to live and the way to respond to the many situations, challenges, and trials that come in a life fully lived. Moreover, with wisdom we find the path to the living God while seeing through the deceptions of the spiritual forces of wickedness and the fallacies of human intellectual endeavor.

Taking the path leading to our Creator and Lord, we then find even greater wisdom, for Proverbs 2:6-7 reminds us of the source of wisdom, knowledge, and understanding. "For the Lord gives wisdom; from His mouth come knowledge and understanding. He stores up sound wisdom for the upright; He is a shield to those who walk in integrity." Life experience surely can make a measure of wisdom and knowledge available to a person. The source of all wisdom and knowledge, however, remains the same as ever it has been. He who created us, breathed life into us, and gave to us our minds with all their capacities is the founder of wisdom and knowledge and the possessor of all wisdom and knowledge.

Why, then, do so many intelligent and learned people deny the existence of our Creator and Lord? That they are lacking in the will to pursue and cultivate wisdom is a significant part of the answer to that question. There is, though, a deep-seated disposition and reality that pulls back and slowly chips away at the will to pursue the fullness of wisdom and ultimate truth. Atheism is a disease of the spirit and heart long before it ever becomes an error of intellect and judgment. Put another way, atheism springs from a spiritual catalyst, not from an intellectual or scientific one. That catalyst is our spiritual adversary whom Jesus identified in John 8:44, Satan, a liar and the father of lies in whom there is no truth. He, whom Jesus identified as "the ruler of this world," is the predominant force in this world for as long as God so allows in accordance with His plan. Thus we can know that Satan and his demonic legions are just as active and influential in the field of academics as in any other. Given the rise of the influence of academia in the modern and postmodern eras, Satanic influence might be stronger there than in most other arenas. Remember, the primary Satanic objective is to turn as many people as possible away from the living God and away from the redemptive work of His Son and Holy Spirt, and to do so by any means that works. As of the past few decades, we can only observe that the American public education system and virtually all institutions of higher education have proven to be an effective means to that end.

When we consider all that has been made manifest to us, that there is a power and moving force within some being far more powerful than anything human or of this world simply cannot be questioned with intellectual integrity. Nor can the fact that there is an intelligence and understanding unfathomable to the greatest capacities of human intellect be rationally questioned. To ask who and what God is can be a rational question and the source of honest and logical debate. The question of whether or not there is a God, however, in mature minds can be neither honest nor logical. Thus David's bold proclamation, "The fool has said in his heart, 'There is no God.'"

The truly wise will seek the living God, simply because of knowing that there is something greater out there if for no other reason. Any man who has a job he likes and desires to hold and who has a modicum of wisdom will try to get to know the head person of his business. Usually his objective is to learn how to please and endear himself to that person so as to maintain both favor and job. At the least, though, he will want to know the boss so as to know how to stay out of his way and avoid disfavor. The most basic reason why the wise will seek the living God is no different than the above occupational analogy.

The wise will seek just because there is something greater. They will seek the one greater so as to know Him, to understand how to gain His favor, or, at the least, to learn how to avoid His disfavor. Are these the most noble of reasons to seek God? Surely not, but they are all logical and wise reasons.

The wise will see the prevalence of evil in this world, and they will discern that there is a relentless spiritual force of darkness behind it. Yet they also will have seen goodness and experienced the effects of righteousness and love. They will realize that what is good, too, has a source, and that the source is a spiritual force beyond what can be seen. This force of light that drives righteousness and lovingkindness and stands firm in the face of evil they will want to know, so they will seek for it. They will search out the light, like a strange evasive star that shines in the darkness.

The wise may also discern the timeless truths of Ecclesiastes. They come to understand that the linear pursuits of all things material and temporal are, in the end, vanity, futility, and striving after the wind. Then a truth much sweeter and to be cherished is realized in Ecclesiastes 3:11.

"He has also set eternity in their heart, yet so that man will not find out the work which God has done from the beginning even to the end." Though the work of our Creator's hands and the specifics of His ultimate plan remain a mystery, the wise understand the reason why they look towards eternity and the sole reason they can even conceive of eternity. They can conceive of eternity because the living God, Creator of all things, has set eternity within the hearts of all people. The concept of eternity and the innate understanding thereof has been put into the hearts of all people, the wise and the unwise alike, by their God. Seeing that "He has made everything appropriate in its time," the wise then know that "He has also set eternity in their heart" for a reason and a time. For eternal life is the intention and desire of God for all people. (1 Pet 3:9). Even without knowledge of Scripture, the wise may seek because of having held an innate understanding of the maxim in Proverbs 15:24. "The path of life leads upward for the wise that he may keep away from Sheol below."

Those truly wise will always seek. They will search as far and wide and for as long as they must. They will follow their "star" wherever it may lead until they enter into the presence of the King of all Kings from whom all wisdom, knowledge, and understanding flow.

To consummate their epiphany, receiving the fullness of wisdom, understanding, peace, and the priceless gift of life that is entrance into the eternal Kingdom, the Magi had to travel far and long. They had to pursue knowledge and truth. They had to leave the comforts and security of home, take risks, endure hardship, and expend of their resources. Spiritually and temporally, they had to cross into the frontiers of the unknown.

Every person's journey will be different. Their "stars"— the light that leads them through earth's darkness—may differ. For some the journey may be long, entailing struggle, risk, effort, trial, and much introspective thought. For others, the journey may be short, with understanding coming to their minds and the peace surpassing all comprehension filling their souls with a minimum of effort. This is wholly natural, as our God has designed us all as individuals. We begin our journeys from different places, hold unique sets of mind and spirit, and may face distinct struggles or challenges.

Regardless of the set and sum of these things in any individual, all whose minds and hearts are open will find a "star" in earth's night. For our God is "He who searches the minds and hearts," and who "will give to each one of you according to your deeds." To all who are open, having the will to seek, He will shine a light that will lead them to the Light that shines eternally in the darkness and that is the life that is "the Light of men."

All who would seek, though, must consider and take to heart the inspired words of the prophet in Jeremiah 29:11-14. "'For I know the plans I have for you,' declares the Lord, 'plans for welfare and not for calamity to give you a future and a hope. Then you will call upon Me and come and pray to Me, and I will listen to you. You will seek Me and find Me when you search for Me with all your heart. I will be found by you,' declares the Lord."

The levels of wisdom, knowledge, and understanding that one receives will be commensurate with the degree to which he has sought. The measure of our Lord's peace and calm assurance bestowed upon you will be correlated with the scope of your search. If you truly desire to find your God and gain significantly in wisdom, knowledge, and the understanding of His Way, you must search for the Lord and strive to know His Way with all your heart and mind. With all capacities, abilities, and resources with which you are blessed, you must seek.

From what is revealed in Scripture, we can know that neither our God nor His beloved Son have ever been impressed by partial commitments or limited efforts.

Perfection they never demanded, but on perfection of effort and fullness of commitment they insisted. Moreover, they always have blessed perfection in effort and fullness of commitment.

Many have claimed to have searched long with all their minds and hearts and to have found nothing. God never appeared to them or revealed anything to them. While I cannot know the depths and truth of the hearts and minds of those proclaiming such to me over the years, I can only note that none of them was convincing. Always I could see clearly a stumbling block or identify shortcomings within the professed searches. The matter, of course, is between each individual and God alone. There I leave it, reminding them that they can fool me or others, but that none can deceive or hide from Him "who searches the minds and hearts." All would do well—believers and nonbelievers alike—to contemplate what it truly means to search with all your heart.

As the new year begins, be wary of complacency. Complacency may not always be sin, but sometimes, at least, it surely is. Just because you have found the salvation and peace of God does not mean that you should cease searching. To the contrary, you should continue to seek Him and His righteousness with each day of life given. No matter how long or how deeply you have held the faith, always you can grow. Let us regularly examine our own hearts and actions against the standard embodied by Christ. Through study, prayer, and meditation, continually seek His Way and His will. Only by so doing can wisdom, knowledge, understanding, and discernment continue to be granted, deepening both the spiritual and temporal intellects.

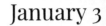

THE LIGHT GOES OUT FROM ISRAEL

> *¹² And having been warned by God in a dream not to return to Herod, the Magi left for their own country by another way.*
>
> Matthew 2:12

The Magi might have had misgivings about returning to begin with. Though we cannot know, they were wise. They were men who had thought of and searched out all things. They were wise to the ways of the world and knew the ways of kings and common people alike, and likely the kind of men who ascertained more from a man's choice of words or merely the language of his body and look in his eyes than was commonly observed. Furthermore, Herod had a reputation that extended well beyond the borders of Judea, as is evident in Augustus' quip that "it was better to be Herod's hog than to be Herod's son."

By one way or another, the Magi may have known that something was not quite right with the king in Jerusalem.

Herod, however, was intelligent, shrewd, and well-spoken. When he so desired, he could be charming and convincing. Such would have been his intention with the Magi. Whatever the inclination of the Magi may have been, divine intervention came upon them for at least a second time and firmly set their course.

The living God who had first come to them far away in Persia with the epiphany now came to them in a dream and warned them not to return to Herod. Just as they had been through the course of their epiphany, the Magi were obedient and left for their own country by another way. Suspecting that Herod had eyes on them and knowing the attention they were sure to attract by all who saw them, they probably left at night under cover of darkness, swinging wide around Jerusalem or heading straight down into the Jordan valley.

Two points herein are worthy of reflection. First, we see again that God will make Himself known to those whose minds and hearts are open. That which is manifested of Him in all creation is given to all, but those whose minds and hearts are open will be visited on more intimate terms. This can be accomplished in a dream, a vision, or an epiphany but can also happen in a myriad of other ways, not the least of which is the all-encompassing counsel of Holy Scripture. The ways of God's communication with His children are limitless, and His capacities for so doing are infinite.

Second, we see herein the divine protection of God being granted through faithful men. In this case, the one being protected by God is His beloved Son. The Magi protect and preserve Jesus' life by choosing to ignore Herod's instructions and leaving Judea surreptitiously.

Our God lacks nothing and needs nothing from human hands. While He has acted and still does act directly to intervene in earthly affairs, for reasons best known to Himself, He most often chooses to enact His will through the actions of people. Whether protecting, providing, encouraging, comforting, admonishing, or punishing, He most often does so by working His will through people. Moreover, He has demonstrated His will to do so using both the righteous and the wicked as well as working through the obedient the same as through the disobedient. He communicated His law to His chosen people through Moses. He conveyed His will, His ways, and His admonishment through the voices of the prophets. He gave to the Israelites the Promised Land, but the men of Israel had to take, hold, and protect it with their own strength at arms. With His covenant broken and His law forsaken, He used the might of the godless nations of Assyria and Babylonia to crush His own chosen people for their unfaithfulness. He healed, encouraged, and made known the path to salvation through Jesus' disciples and apostles. He gave them power and understanding, but they still had to go out and do the work. The examples are many, and so it would appear that our God prefers to work the preponderance of His will through human action and occasionally even through animals (Ex 7-10; Num 21-22; 2 Kgs 2; Dan 6).

Thus, like the Magi, our minds and hearts must remain open. We must be aware of His working within us and remain cognizant of His instruction to us and His will for us. Such may be revealed in Scripture, through prayer and meditation, or by some other medium in the daily walk of life. By remaining open and willing, we keep within our minds and before our eyes the importance of our actions taken on behalf of others. For each person who lives and serves in accordance with the will of God is doing the work of God by putting action to His divine plan . This action may take the form of protecting, providing, comforting, encouraging, nurturing, mentoring, teaching, correcting, peacemaking, or admonishing. All, when properly applied, is the work of our Lord. For all who would faithfully follow Christ, our duty is to do that work to the best of our ability in accordance with

His will in all situations. Therein is to be found our simple and timeless, yet often difficult and trying, purpose in living. As Sakamoto Ryoma put it, "The purpose of coming into the world is to accomplish one's duty."

With minds and hearts open, the Magi heard the truth of God, acted in obedience, and fulfilled their duty before Him from the onset of their journey to their last glance toward the north as they rode out of Bethlehem in the night. Here, as they begin the long ride back to Persia, reflections upon the Magi generally end. While we are told nothing more of them in Scripture, however, there may be much still worthy of consideration.

Beyond the obvious—that they returned to their homes in Persia—where else did they go from here? What did they do? What, if anything, was different from their daily routines prior to the culmination of the epiphany? How were their lives changed? Having been given such an epiphany and then to have looked into the eternal eyes of the Son of God beneath the guiding star, we can be sure that there was change. Knowledge and understanding not of this world had been bestowed upon them and the divine guidance of the star had proven to be true. Mindset and commitment of the heart could never be the same as before. What, then, did they reveal to others along their travels and at home? Such an experience and unprecedented revelation was unlikely to be kept a lifelong secret. With their closest friends and peers, at least, we can imagine the long nights of conversation in lamplight or under the stars of Persia's night. The experience revealed, the reflection, the questions, the contemplations, and the speculation all likely played out many times over. Presuming that such did occur, what was the impact of the story and new-found knowledge and understanding of the Magi upon those who listened? Though we can likely never know on this side of Heaven, in it all is to be found fertile ground for contemplation and reflection.

There are some things of significance, however, that we can know. In the divine calling of the Magi, the epiphany given them, and in their coming, going, and leaving of telling gifts is revealed what was to be the nature of the new covenant. The new covenant of which the prophet Jeremiah spoke, unlike the old covenant that had long been broken, would be put within the children of God and written upon their hearts, and He would forgive their iniquity and remember their sin no more. The covenant would be bought and sealed by the blood of only one atoning sacrifice for all people. The "Righteous One," foreseen by the prophet Isaiah, would bear the iniquities and carry the sorrows of all, being "pierced through" for the transgressions of all people and "crushed" for their iniquities that the many might be justified before their God. Remember that the gift of myrrh revealed a clear understanding that an ultimate sacrifice must be offered, and would be given, on behalf of all people.

Further, we see fulfillment of the call in Isaiah 49 to the distant "islands" and to "peoples from afar." For from Israel would go out a "light of the nations" so that the salvation of God would "reach to the end of the earth." Too, we begin to see already the fulfillment of the bondservant Simeon's prophecy in the temple from Luke 2. "For my eyes have seen Your salvation, which You have prepared in the presence of all peoples, a Light of revelation to the gentiles."

For it was unto gentiles—the Persian Magi—that this epiphany had been given. With the depth of understanding granted them therein of the nature of the redemptive plan of God for all people, there is a very real sense in which the Gospel Light of Jesus Christ, the Messiah, went out from Israel to the East with the Magi. Jesus' gospel, of course, was yet to be proclaimed. However, we cannot look full upon the experience and actions of the Magi and consider the divine intervention that so clearly penetrated their minds and hearts and set before their eyes a miraculous guiding star and not see, at least, an embryonic form of the gospel taking root within open minds and hearts and being carried eastward with understanding and words of hope, peace, and salvation for all people. This King would rule not only in Judea but would rule all kingdoms and domains to the ends of the earth forevermore. The kingdom of this King was not of this world, and this kingdom would welcome those of every nation, tribe, and tongue.

Just as the divine light of a star had guided the Magi on the long journey from the East to Him who was the Light of men that shines in the darkness, so the divine Light of men, which would become the gospel, went out of Israel to the East. The Light was carried in the hearts of the Magi; an understanding of the path to redemption and peace with God for all people through the atoning sacrifice of the King of Kings soon to come. Though not yet in its completed form, the salvific understanding being carried eastward was unprecedented and revolutionary in the spheres of human spirituality and religion.

Of kings and kingdoms this world knew. The concept of blood atonement not only was almost universally understood but was, and long had been, widely practiced throughout the ancient world. Sacrificial bloodletting had not been confined to animals alone. Human blood, too, had been spilled and would continue to be shed upon many altars just as it also had been quenched of life by consuming fires. Yet this world had never conceived of a King who would shed His own lifeblood as the atoning sacrificial offering for all people of every nation, tribe, and tongue. Only in the prophetic utterances of David and Isaiah are to be found the foreshadowings of such a sacrifice, but the concept was realized or accepted by few even among the most devout of the Covenant. Nor had there ever been conceived or proposed a kingdom without borders or end with entrance therein determined not by ethnicity, birth, status, or deed but solely by the disposition of one's heart. Never had it been conceived that the willing sacrifice of One, wholly righteous, would forever bridge the gap over the otherwise impassable gulf between God and men. With their epiphany, however, and its culmination of having looked into the living eyes of eternity in the face of the Christ Child, the Magi understood this. With this unprecedented spiritual understanding they rode back toward their Persian homeland.

We might see in the quest of the Magi, then, something of a corollary with the life and mission of John the Baptist. John, as is revealed in the first chapter of Luke's gospel, was given life for the purpose of preparing himself to be, and then fulfilling the role of, a forerunner before Jesus, "so as to make ready a people prepared for the Lord." John would go out before Jesus to prepare the minds and hearts of the people for a new way of thinking and for greater understanding. He would "go on before the Lord to prepare His ways; to give His people the knowledge of salvation by the forgiveness of their sins."

Clearly there are differences between the life and mission of John and the lives of the Magi. Furthermore, we have textual accounts of John's actions while we have none of the Magi beyond that of Matthew 2. Yet if we consider the role of a forerunner and ponder the nature of what must be possessed and understood to enable one in that capacity, a striking commonality may be perceived.

Divine intervention touched John's life from conception. Divine inspiration was upon him from the beginning, as he was "filled with the Holy Spirit while yet in his mother's womb." By divine inspiration he was given knowledge and understanding that other people did not have. Such had to be given him so that he knew what to say and do to "make ready a people prepared for the Lord." The Way of Jesus would constitute a new way of thinking and living. John had to know something of these new ways so as to be able to articulate them to the people who understood nothing of the Messiah to follow in his steps.

Divine intervention, likewise, came upon the Magi in the form of their epiphany. That which was revealed to them about the divine King to be born, their calling to follow the star in the western sky until they found Him and then in the dream when God told them not to return to Herod. Thus the Magi rode out of Judea with an understanding of what was to be the new covenant of the gospel of the Son of the living God and an understanding surpassing that of virtually all other people upon the earth. Zacharias, Elizabeth, Joseph, Mary, Simeon, Anna, and a few shepherds may have understood as much. Most Jews, however, still thought of the coming Messiah solely in Jewish terms and focused upon what was to be accomplished by Him for Israel's sake alone. Though there were spiritual expectations among the more devout, the prevailing emphasis was the expectation of a warrior king like David—though greater than David— who would restore the earthly kingdom and push back and subdue their enemies. Had they examined the words of their own prophets more closely, openly, and objectively, though, they would have seen in the Messiah to come something quite different.

In Isaiah 7:14 they would have foreseen a King not of this world who would be Immanuel, born of a virgin. In Psalm 22 and Isaiah 53, not a king leading armies out to war but a suffering servant who would be pierced through and crushed for the transgressions and iniquities of all people and who would bear and carry our griefs and sorrows. Then in Isaiah 49 they would have seen the Messiah of Israel who also would be a light of the nations so that His salvation would go out to all people to the ends of the earth.

What the Magi carried out of Bethlehem was a messianic understanding that had eluded most Jews and was wholly unknown in the vast gentile world beyond. Being gentiles themselves and knowing that the living God had called out to them, granted them understanding, and then had guided them, they realized that the God of Israel was not only for Israel but was the God of all people and all creation. They understood that the King sent down from Heaven by Him would offer the atoning sacrifice not only for Israel but for all people to the ends of the earth. They discerned that His Kingdom would be opened up to all people who would believe in Him and call upon Him as Lord, that it would be a spiritual kingdom and not a temporal one, and that it would be established unto everlasting.

While John went out among the chosen in Israel as a forerunner to prepare their minds and hearts for Jesus' message of repentance and truth, the Magi went out as forerunners among the gentiles in the East. That the Magi were given the epiphany, that they were called, and that they were guided to the Christ Child was, in itself, a signal from God that the atoning sacrifice of His beloved Son and the salvation to be granted thereby was to be for all people. Beyond that, however, even though we have no textual account, we can presume that the Magi themselves became the forerunners in the East to prepare minds for a new way of thinking and hearts for a new understanding. For as they related their epiphany, their experience, and their new understanding, the Way of our Lord would begin to be made known and a people prepared for the Lord would begin to be made ready.

The ways of our God are not the ways of men, and in His ways much will remain a mystery. Yet we can know that in all His ways and actions there is a purpose and a plan. Always, by many methods and manifestations, He has made Himself known to men, and always He will continue to do so. Those who seek with all their hearts will find Him. Those whose minds and hearts are truly open will be found by Him.

THE ANGEL AND THE FLIGHT TO EGYPT

[13] Now when they had gone, behold, an angel of the Lord appeared to Joseph in a dream and said, "Get up! Take the Child and His mother and flee to Egypt, and remain there until I tell you; for Herod is going to search for the Child to destroy Him." [14] So Joseph got up and took the Child and His mother while it was still night, and left for Egypt. [15] He remained there until the death of Herod. This was to fulfill what had been spoken by the Lord through the prophet: "Out of Egypt I called My Son."

Matthew 2:13-15

Two aspects of this passage emerge for reflection. First, we see the importance of Joseph as the man chosen to be the earthly father of our Lord and the head of His home. Second, the temporal purpose of the gifts presented by the Magi becomes clear.

Angels remain prominent in our decorations, songs, films, stories, and discussions throughout the Christmas season, and for good reason. The angelic role in the Advent of our Lord was significant. Beginning in verse thirteen, though, we should note and remember a pattern that is consistent throughout Scripture.

Many are fascinated by angels, and for some, that fascination can border upon obsession. Others constantly look for angels in the mysterious, unknown strangers who suddenly appear, for example, or wonder why they do not seem to manifest themselves as often today as they did in biblical times. While I can offer no proof, I believe they are just as active in our world today as they have ever been, and in particular situations they do still make themselves manifest.

However, angels do not appear to entertain or to prove a point. They act when all human resources and capacities have been exhausted and when human abilities, knowledge, or understanding are simply not sufficient to comprehend what must be done in accordance with the will of God. For this reason the angel appeared to Joseph in his dream. Joseph, though an obedient servant of God, had no way of knowing what Herod's reaction would be after the Magi slipped covertly out of Judea. So the angel came, commanding him to "Get up!" and take Jesus and Mary to Egypt and remain there until he was told it was safe to return.

Though Joseph is often overlooked in our Christmas-time remembrances, being reduced to little more than a requisite figure in the creches of the world with the focus upon Jesus, Mary, the angels, and perhaps the shepherds and Magi, this should not be so. For just as God did not act randomly or lightly in choosing the mother who would give birth to and nurture our Lord, neither did He choose at random or by whim the man who would be His father, protector, provider, and teacher in the ways of the world.

Mary was chosen because in her righteousness, faithfulness, and humility she found favor with God. We can presume nothing less in God's choice of Joseph. Yet to be a faithful husband and father in the way of our

God, still more is required. Such a man must be gentle in love, just in judgments, decisive in leadership, and fierce in protection. Joseph already had demonstrated his gentleness, lovingkindness, and a sense of justice and fairness; but now the situation shifts for the worse. The life of his young son and perhaps his wife also are in imminent danger. Soldiers are coming to kill Him.

Joseph asked no questions. He did not open the matter for discussion. He did not hesitate and did not waiver. He awoke Mary and Jesus, quickly gathered their meager possessions, and took them out of the house under the cover of night and started toward Egypt.

Not by any coincidence had God chosen as the earthly father to His Son a strong and courageous man with the blood of warriors running in his veins. Though never a soldier himself, Joseph was a descendant of the valiant warriors of Judah in the House of David. Courage and strength were innate to his constitution. Thus the decisiveness of his response and his indomitable will to protect his own, and thus the reason he neither flinched nor vacillated at taking his family out into the night and traveling far and long into an unknown situation and future. He alone of this earth would be provider and protector for his wife and Son, and it was a duty and burden that he took up and carried without hesitation or complaint, even without knowing what the days and weeks ahead would hold.

Joseph, however, did not set off for Egypt empty-handed. A staff—the common multipurpose walking stick, an effective blade or two, perhaps a few carpentry tools, and the clothes on his back would have comprised the bulk of his possessions. Yet now, by the providence of God and the obedience and generosity of the Magi, he carried with him the valuable commodities of gold, frankincense, and myrrh, all of which could be turned over for cash or put to barter.

There had been no time to plan or prepare. Already, due to political circumstances and the unforeseeable plan of God, he had been forced to make do and provide for his family in Bethlehem far from his home and base of business in Nazareth. Then, in a matter of minutes, he had to leave not only for another city but for another country where culture, language, customs, and laws would all be different. There he would have to find housing and provide for his family.

The substantial monetary value of the gifts of the Magi not only made this possible but also meant that the transition, aside from the long journey over the desert, could be a relatively comfortable one. Shelter, food, clothing, medicine, and basic supplies could be secured for a substantial period with profits from the sale of the frankincense and myrrh and the purchasing power of the gold, which was generally as good in and of itself as any currency. Though we do not know the duration of the family's stay in Egypt, their funds also would have been sufficient for Joseph to obtain whatever tools or supplies he needed to establish himself in business had he deemed that necessary.

Whatever course of action Joseph took, it seems safe to presume that he prospered and that the family had a comfortable and secure life in Egypt, suggesting the reason that Egyptian Christians have long taken pride in their country's role in providing refuge for our Lord in the time of trouble. From what can be inferred in the latter verses of the chapter, Joseph appears to have been in no hurry to get out of Egypt. The angel found him there in peaceful sleep, having remained just as he had been told to do in the angel's previous appearance. Furthermore, Joseph, though he immediately obeyed, seems to have been calculating and unhurried upon the family's return to Israel. Concerned again of the safety of his young Son, he thought it best to avoid the vicinity of Jerusalem—including Bethlehem—which would have been a closer destination than the Galilee region.

When his concerns were verified by God in another dream, he took the longer journey up into Galilee.

What can be known with certainty is that the gifts of the Magi covered the family's expenses for their resettlement in a foreign land. For a young father and mother who already had been through much trial and struggle, God, working through genuine seekers from afar, had provided in abundance for their immediate worldly needs. In no way does the fact lessen the spiritual significance of the gold, frankincense, and myrrh. Rather, it simply makes clear that the gifts had both a spiritual and a temporal purpose. Of the two, the spiritual aspect was of greatest import. For therein was revealed what was to be the nature, purpose, and role of the newborn King. The temporal aspect of the gifts, as they eased what would have been a tremendous burden following a difficult couple years, serves as a reminder of the importance of giving and how God so often works through select people to meet the needs of other people. More specifically, there is a reminder of the virtue and value of thoughtful giving.

To give a gift with forethought and purpose is a concept either not understood or never considered by many. Simply to give indiscriminately merely for the sake of giving is neither virtuous nor in line with biblical precepts. For example, to give a drunkard on the street the money for his next bottle accomplishes nothing for good. To give a nice gift to a person known to be lacking in character, maturity, and a proper appreciation and who would likely squander the gift or never put it to appropriate use would, in most cases, be an errant choice lacking both discernment and virtue.

The old adage that, "what matters most in a gift is the thought behind it," generally holds true, and every gift should be received with this mindset. A good and meaningful gift, however, is one that has been thought out and chosen based upon the needs, circumstances, desires, or inclinations of the recipient. Yet the best gifts—those which will carry the greatest significance and meaning—are the ones considered and selected according to the aforementioned criteria but that hold spiritual significance as well as practical application.

Such a gift could be many very different things and is neither limited nor validated by the purchase price. The spiritual significance of certain items is sufficiently obvious. A cross, a menorah, or a framed passage of Scripture speak for themselves. Yet many other objects, which in and of themselves have no religious meaning at all, might have great spiritual meaning to an individual because the spiritual significances of things can often be determined by one's life experience. Likewise, the practical application value of a gift can also be determined by life experience or way of living.

Because my wife knows my innermost thoughts, she knows that if she gives me a new sword, she has not only given me something of material value that will be used but also something that holds great spiritual significance to me. When I give a young man the gift of a sword, I am giving him a weapon with a martial application. First and foremost, however, I am giving him a gift that is spiritual and that is meant to serve as a constant reminder to him of the Word of God and of his duties as a man set forth in Scripture. When I select a piece of jewelry as a gift for my wife, I look for something that I think she would enjoy wearing, but seldom only that. In most cases, either the wording that forms the piece, the symbol or symbols thereon, the materials from which it is composed, or some combination of all is selected to set before her mind and heart something good, pleasant, comforting, challenging, or that will constantly remind her of my deepest devotion. Sometimes no expenditure is required and little effort is necessary. While on the beach at Marathon where the Persian forces landed in 490 B.C. to do battle with the Athenians, my wife picked up a small stone which she later gave to me at dinner that night. The stone has neither beauty nor monetary value. Yet to me, she knew it would be treasured, as it would be a reminder of our shared experience together and of the culmination of years of spiritual, physical, and intellectual endeavor on my part.

The best gifts always are those chosen with thoughtfulness and purpose. Paramount among these, then, are those which combine the attributes of the spiritual and the temporal. Not every gift given need be such, for there are different kinds of gifts just as there are various relationships, occasions, and protocols. Nevertheless, amid this season when we so often think of giving gifts, the gifts of the Magi, holding profound spiritual significance while also being pragmatic and of earthly value, are worthy of reflection.

Fortified by the gifts of the Magi, Joseph and Mary made a home in Egypt and remained there until Herod's death. The passage ends with the words of the Lord as given to the prophet Hosea: "Out of Egypt I called My Son." Matthew knew well that the words of Hosea 11:1 referred to Israel's exodus from Egypt, but he also understood the foreknowledge of God in in all things. Just as Moses had delivered the children of Israel from captivity in Egypt, so one like Moses but greater than Moses must come to establish a new covenant and deliver people from slavery to sin, to defeat the works of Satan, and conquer the power of death. Under divine inspiration as he wrote, Matthew knew that that deliverer, destroyer of Satan's schemes, and conqueror of death had been revealed in Jesus, beloved and only begotten Son of God. So just as He had called His son Israel out of Egypt and to the Promised Land more than a thousand years before, now He called His Son Jesus Messiah out of Egypt to lead all who would follow into the promised land that is the eternal Kingdom of God.

Nearing the end of this season in which so many gifts are exchanged and looking to the year ahead, consider deeply the gifts you will give and the impact that may be had upon those receiving them. Reflect upon what you might give to ease the burdens of others, meet specific needs, to help them reach an objective, develop a new skill, increase in learning and wisdom, or open their eyes and minds to something new. Think especially about gifts with both spiritual significance and practical application so as to keep before your eyes and in your mind spiritual principles and truths while still being physically utilized or enjoyed.

Remember, too, that you need not wait for the coming of Christmas or birthdays to give gifts. The giving of good and purposeful gifts in any time and place is but a natural outgrowth inherent to walking in the Way of Christ. Giving should spring innately from the lovingkindness, empathy, compassion, and hospitality Jesus embodied and taught.

When I was young, there was an older man who filled the role as a sort of third grandfather to me. We hunted together, travelled together, and I sometimes worked for him during the summer months. Once, on a summer road trip down to the Mexican border, he reached behind his truck seat and handed me a brand new knife. Thrilled, of course, I began to examine all parts of it closely. Then, realizing there was no special occasion insofar as I was aware, I inquired as to the reason for such a nice gift. His answer has remained close in my mind through the many years since.

While saying that he had no problem with the giving of gifts at Christmas or on special occasions, he noted that he never gave much thought to it. Rather, he explained, whenever he saw something that brought a particular person to his mind, he would purchase it then and there and give it to him the next time they met. "That's my philosophy on gifts," he added in summary. Whatever may be one's personal philosophy on the giving of gifts, in the gifts of the Magi coupled with the Way of Christ, there is something to be taken by us all.

Finally, and especially for men of all ages, do not miss or fail to contemplate the importance of manhood and fatherhood as revealed in this brief passage. Just as God did not choose lightly or at whim the man who would be the earthly father of His Son, nor has He lightly or flippantly assigned the duties of manhood and fatherhood to all reasonably able-bodied men. We live in a culture and time in which those with power and influence degrade, mock, and strive to neuter genuine manhood while pushing to marginalize and geld fatherhood. This renders it all the more imperative that the lessons from Joseph be taken and internalized.

Husbands and fathers bear the God-given duty to lead by action always and by word when necessary. They must be strong spiritually, mentally, and physically. They are to be protectors, guarding their wives and their children in the face of all dangers and protecting also those others around them who may be unable to protect themselves. They must be savvy to the ways of the world. Know the dangers, pitfalls, and snares and know the nature and end of life's different paths and roads. Then, embodying all this, they must be gentle, loving, and just. From the time of Mary's conception through the flight to, and return from, Egypt, Joseph embodied all these attributes. In a culture bent on the evisceration of manhood and the neutralization of fatherhood, Joseph's life and actions provide a model and standard for which all men should strive.

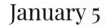

January 5

TWO KINGS AND TWO EMPTY TOMBS

> *16 Then when Herod saw that he had been tricked by the Magi, he became very enraged, and sent and slew all the male children who were in Bethlehem and all its vicinity, from two years old and under, according to the time which he had determined from the Magi. 17 Then what had been spoken through Jeremiah the prophet was fulfilled:*
>
> > *18 "A voice was heard in Ramah,*
> > *Weeping and great mourning,*
> > *Rachel weeping for her children;*
> > *And she refused to be comforted,*
> > *Because they were no more."*
>
> Matthew 2:16-18

Little inspiration is to be had by turning our focus upon a man as wicked as Herod the king during the joyous season of Christmas; or so it may seem with but a passing thought. Indeed, his bent toward evil and his paranoia-driven bloodshed remain indisputable despite even the current efforts of some Israeli scholars to rehabilitate his image through stillborn revisions of history. One such scholar, remarkably, appeared to lament the king's length of years, noting that if only Herod had died ten years earlier, or if more of his sons had died prematurely of natural causes, history would have remembered the great king more favorably. Had such been the case, he never would have felt the necessity of murdering three of his own sons, not to mention the host of others killed at his orders through that final decade.

Whether such attempts at scholarship are more comical or more egregious is difficult to say. If a frog had wings, we may suppose that he would not bump his backside when he hopped. Dispensing with revisionist longings and sentimental what-ifs, the fact is that Herod did live those infamous ten years, and he did murder three of his own sons. Another fact is that his propensity for bloodshed was verifiably demonstrated long before his final decade. He killed his Hasmonean wife Mariamne, her mother Alexandra, her brother Aristobulus III, and her grandfather Hyrcanus II well before this time. As bloody as it is, the above list is nowhere near exhaustive.

Wishful thinking aside, all of a man's years are counted by both men and by God. Furthermore, it is not at all unusual for the inclinations of a man's heart, be they for the better of for the worse, to be revealed more fully through action and word in later years. Herod had been ruthless and wicked through all his years. The only futile effort at his defense would have to rest in the supposition that the paranoia fueled by dissipation and the ravages of age served to exacerbate his already ruthless inclinations. Nevertheless, there remains no defense for the indefensible.

Despite his utter wickedness, Herod remains as central to the story of Christ's birth as any other person, and for two reasons. First, he held the power in Judea at the time. The Roman imperium was the ultimate authority, but so long as

Herod proved useful to the Romans they were content to leave the internal affairs of his kingdom to his discretion.

Second, in the person and actions of Herod can be most readily seen a vessel of the spiritual forces of wickedness Jesus came to engage and destroy. He did not come to do battle with Herod or his descendants, for they were but the vessels of the true adversary. He came to counter and smash the designs of the Satanic forces of darkness that ruled them and the world they inhabited.

There are two ways by which a man may prove to be an effective teacher. One lies in proclaiming by word and demonstrating through actions the right things to do. The other way is by demonstrating all the wrong actions and suffering the consequences, thereby unwittingly revealing the reasons why the choice of doing right is a wiser one. Likewise, we may sometimes gain more perspective of the blessings and virtue of the ever-challenging pursuit of righteousness by considering the consequences suffered by those who lived in iniquity, pursuing only the wealth, pleasures, power, and glory of the temporal world through a fleeting vapor of life. The destructive consequences made manifest throughout and in the end of a life given to greed, debauchery, and bloodshed can prove more illuminating of the virtues and blessings of a life lived in pursuit of righteousness and truth than might a well-delivered sermon.

In Herod, we are invited to observe and consider the inverse of the Way of Christ. For all who truly follow Him, Herod is the antithesis of everything that we cherish and celebrate at Christmas. To fully appreciate the message Jesus delivered, the actions He demonstrated, and the demands He made of us, we must reckon with the consequences and ends of Herod's life and those of any life expended in pursuit of all things counter to the ways of our Lord. In the juxtaposition of opposites, facts have a way of speaking for themselves. For in their ends of earthly life, Jesus and Herod shared one noteworthy fact in common. Both left an empty tomb, but the manner by which the tombs were emptied was markedly different and eternally revealing.

Herod was born of an Idumean father and a Nabataean mother. Most in Judea considered him to be only a half-Jew at best, and some allowed not even for that. The blood of hardened men of the deserts to the south and east coursed through his veins. Contrary to common depictions in film, he was not always the profligate, fat, and sickly slob portrayed. As a young man he was strong, a formidable fighter, and a natural and energetic leader of men. He was a man either to be stepped aside from or to be approached with sword sharpened and ready.

Herod's view of himself was as a king in the Hellenistic tradition. He gravitated quite naturally to the Roman lifestyle not only because Rome was the true power in the region but also for the fact that he enjoyed it. For Roman baths, swimming pools, wine, parties, palaces, and other amenities he held a notable fondness. Ideals of moderation, discipline, and self-control common in the days of the Republic he surely held to in certain facets of his life if not in others.

Much influenced by what he saw of Roman architecture, Herod became a great builder. He was, in fact, unarguably the greatest builder in Judean history. Monuments to his genius, creativity and skill span the country still today. At his palace atop the natural fortress of Masada, for example, ruins suggest that he may have built the world's first infinity pool.

As notable as were his intellect and skills, so, too, were his patterns of ruthlessness and brutality. Where and when violence could serve his ends, only the restraints of politics, which generally meant being sure not to upset Rome, could turn him from it. As energetically as he worked to secure his kingdom and pursue his building projects, he ventured with equal enthusiasm and increasing frequency into the Roman-style party scene. He was an avid entertainer and, by Roman standards, a splendid host. That is to say that he could throw a good party, and there is little to suggest that he did not much enjoy the pleasures of sensuality and wine himself.

The cocktail of unchecked greed and unrestrained indulgence can be lethal in and of itself, both physically and spiritually. That alone could have proven Herod's ruin. When penchants for bloodshed and possession of absolute power are added to the mix, the lethality is magnified, both to the individual and to the people surrounding him, and the devastation and scope of all ruined is greater still.

The cumulative deleterious effect of it all began to show in Herod. As his body started to deteriorate to become fatter, weaker, more sickly, and but a shell of the strong man he once had been, his mind degenerated into a frenzied paranoia and deranged obsession with holding on to his power and his kingdom regardless of whose blood or how much blood had to be shed. Therein lay a great irony and the vividly embodied truth of the destruction wreaked within the human mind and heart by iniquity. Even as Herod realized his mortality and slipped steadily toward death's door, he schemed, fought, and murdered to try and hold on to that which intellectually he knew well he never could retain. He pressed and killed to secure crown and kingdom, to hold them in an iron grip that he knew was about to be forever relaxed by death.

Yet even as death put about Herod the slowly tightening chokehold that would take him to his grave, he set in motion the plan for his most spectacular murder. If successful, this murder, though he could not have known it, would impact the world forever. For it would cut short the life of the only one holding the knowledge and power to change the world once and for all time. No threat to his kingdom and dynasty could be overlooked, not even that of a newborn baby to a poor family of Judah. He had only now to await word from the Magi. As we have seen, though, God's angel intervened. The Magi did not return to Herod, and Joseph took Mary and Jesus to safety in Egypt.

Herod, of course, was enraged at the Magi's ruse. Thus he set his plan in motion, only on a much larger scale. Based upon the appearance of the strange star as related to him by the Magi, he concluded that the newborn King of the Jews could not possibly be more than two years old and was likely significantly younger. So he gave his soldiers the order for all male children two years and younger to be put to the sword on that dark night as Joseph, not yet far away, led his family toward the sanctuary of Egypt.

Shortly thereafter, as the ever-tightening squeeze of death resigned Herod to his end, he laid the plans for the most extravagant funeral Judea had ever seen. Just outside the village of Bethlehem on the slope of one of his grandest palaces, the Herodium, he had built a magnificent and highly ornamented mausoleum of stone to be his eternal resting place. He had ordered the making of a beautiful red limestone sarcophagus, smoothed and polished so it appeared as fine marble.

Though blinded by paranoia and the veil of iniquity, Herod held no illusions with regard to the feelings of most in Judea about his imminent death. That few would mourn him and that none in his own family would shed a tear, he was well aware. To ensure that there would be tears, genuine sorrow, and much mourning, he had a number of the most respected Jewish leaders arrested and confined in the hippodrome at Jericho and ordered his sister Salome to have them killed immediately upon his death.

That part of the funeral plans would be spoiled, for as soon as Herod died in Jericho, Salome ordered the release of all the Jewish prisoners. Thus the initial rejoicing of the people was twofold and magnified. The funerary procession itself was ordered in accordance with Herod's desires.

Aside from Herod's dry-eyed family, Josephus reports that his entire army outfitted for battle, and five hundred of his servants were among the procession that marched to the sounds of trumpets and eulogies from Jericho all the way up to the mausoleum he had prepared at Herodium outside of Bethlehem. Herod was dressed in his finery and a crown of gold and was carried the entire distance upon a bier of solid gold ornamented with precious stones. There below the great palace-fortress, but a few miles from the small cave in which Jesus had entered the world, Herod was put into the shiny sarcophagus of red limestone and laid to rest in splendor.

The Child now growing in Egypt, whom he had sought to kill to secure that which he could never hold, was soon to return. Within the Child's short life, the kingdom of Herod would be erased forever, lost to direct Roman rule. In the Roman province of Palestine, the Child, grown to the prime of manhood, would demonstrate the actions of love that resonate still today. He would preach a message that moved and changed the hearts of men and women and shook the foundations of the world. He would finish His life by giving it up on a Roman cross for the sins of Herod and those of every other person, the wicked and the righteous.

He had no servants and no army to attend His funeral. He had no clothes save for the simple garments that had been bartered among soldiers as He hung and died. There was no bier upon which He could be carried. As He had possessed no money, He had no tomb to be prepared for His eternal rest. A small, nondescript tomb was given for His burial by another man. So insignificant was His allotted place of burial that we cannot know with certainty exactly where it is today.

Though a cause of great sorrow and mourning then among His devoted followers in Jerusalem, we know now that all was well. He would not need the small space for long.

A stone was placed and sealed over the tomb, and a guard was posted at the request of the chief priests and Pharisees. They could guard the sealed tomb with an armed force superior to any that the grieving and scattered followers could bring against it.

They put before the tomb all they thought was needed, but on the third day, the seal had been broken and the stone moved away. All who crouched and entered found the small tomb empty. No body was ever found, not by His followers, the chief priests, the Pharisees, or the Romans. No body would be found, but the Man would appear again before His own, embracing, speaking, eating and giving final instructions. His tomb, wherever it may be, is empty still today. The sacrifice of atonement made and the promise fulfilled, He awaits all who have followed Him in righteousness.

In 2007, after a search of many years, Israeli archaeologist Ehud Netzer discovered Herod's tomb on the slope of Herodium outside Bethlehem. He and a number of other archaeologists and scholars, it should be noted, have done outstanding work both in excavation and in preparing all that was found for exhibit to the public in the Israel Museum. In the years before professor Netzer's discovery, I had several times walked very close to Herod's royal resting place, never having any idea that anything was there just below the surface of the slope upon which I climbed. The reason that I saw nothing, as it turned out, was that the magnificent mausoleum had been smashed at the hands of men, reduced to rubble, and overtaken by the soil of the Judean hills.

What Professor Netzer discovered in the rubble was a long empty tomb-just as void of any human remains as had been the tomb of Jesus after three days. For scattered amid the shattered and crushed stone he found, in literally hundreds of small pieces, all that was left of what once had been a beautiful, highly polished sarcophagus of red limestone. He thought it had been the one in which the great king had been laid to rest by the telling fact that it had been so deliberately and thoroughly destroyed.

By his estimation, the entire structure stood for no longer than seventy years. Destruction came at the hands of a few among the myriad of those who still hated the great king and any remaining reminder of him. Followers of the Christ Child whom Herod had sought so desperately to kill, however, were not among those who wrought the destruction. The tomb had been emptied and then reduced by Jewish rebels in the early stages of the revolt against the Romans who then ruled the great king's land.

Herod and Jesus both left behind empty tombs, but the manners in which, and the ends to which, they were emptied were as different as the night is from the day. Indeed, the two men were as opposite in life as is the darkness from the light. Just a miniscule percentage of the population ever to have lived has read the biography of Herod to be found in four volumes of Flavius Josephus' Jewish Antiquities. The Holy Bible, which holds the story and teachings of the life of Jesus Christ, is the best-selling and most widely distributed book in the history of the world. The name of Jesus is known to the ends of the earth, and forever it will be known. The relatively few who know the name of Herod know it only from their readings of the miraculous birth of the Bethlehem Child. The kingdom of Herod passed like a fleeting vapor. The kingdom of God under the reign of our Lord Jesus Christ has been established unto everlasting even as still it grows, welcoming the faithful of every nation, tribe, and tongue.

FINAL REFLECTIONS

¹⁹ But when Herod died, behold, an angel of the Lord appeared in a dream to Joseph in Egypt, and said, ²⁰ "Get up, take the Child and His mother, and go into the land of Israel; for those who sought the Child's life are dead." ²¹ So Joseph got up, took the Child and His mother, and came into the land of Israel. ²² But when he heard that Archelaus was reigning over Judea in place of his father Herod, he was afraid to go there. Then after being warned by God in a dream, he left for the regions of Galilee, ²³ and came and lived in a city called Nazareth. This was to fulfill what was spoken through the prophets: "He shall be called a Nazarene."

Matthew 2:19-23

An angel of the Lord came again to Joseph in a dream with the news of Herod's death, commanding him to leave Egypt and return to the land of Israel. Being warned by God in another dream along the way confirmed his suspicions about the safety of Jerusalem, thus Joseph stayed well to the west and took Mary and Jesus north into Galilee where they settled in the small city of Nazareth. "This was to fulfill what was spoken through the prophets: 'He shall be called a Nazarene.'"

This last phrase of chapter two has long been a favorite target of those desiring to prove the errancy of Holy Scripture. Such efforts, of course, have been as determined as they have been unrelenting. Attacks upon Judeo-Christian Scripture will continue and likely will intensify amid the current degeneration of culture, backlash against organized religion, burgeoning anti-Semitism, and the growing hostility towards Christians and all expressions of the Christian faith.

As we observe this final day of the Christmas season and reflect upon the epiphany of the newborn King whose Kingdom, having neither borders nor end of days, will welcome people of every nation, tribe, and tongue, let His peace fill your soul and fret not about opposition and hostility. Though it may seem a dichotomy, there is a certain comfort and blessed assurance to be taken by all genuine believers in the face of such opposition. Recall the prophecy of Simeon when the Holy Spirit came upon him in the temple as he held the baby Jesus in his arms. "For my eyes have seen Your salvation…A light of revelation to the Gentiles, and the glory of Your people Israel…Behold, this Child is appointed for the fall and rise of many in Israel, and for a sign to be opposed."

Our Lord Jesus Christ came in Advent as a sign to be opposed. Thus any opposition to Him, to His Word, or to His followers is merely the fulfillment of what was prophesied from the beginning. The reality is that it could not be any other way.

Satan, with his spiritual forces of wickedness in the heavenly places, is the ruler of this world. Jesus Himself referred to him as such multiple times. Thus the predominant ways of this world are the ways inspired and driven by the forces of Satan's darkness. The prevailing currents flow as he moves them.

Amid this prevalence of darkness and deception, one cannot speak the truth in all things and not be opposed. Never in any era or place has it been possible to speak in full of spiritual truth particularly and not meet some level of opposition. Despite His demonstrations of supernatural power and His embodiment of gentleness, love, and compassion for all people, even Jesus could not speak truth without meeting the most extreme manifestations of opposition. So long as evil remains the dominant force in this world, truth never will be unopposed.

Aside from the Satanic catalyst behind the opposition, though, there is another prominent factor that has remained unchanged from the beginning. The power and legitimacy in the name and person of Jesus are innately felt, or sensed, by all people and, thus, are understood by all. Levels of understanding vary, as some can articulate the specifics of biblical doctrines while others cannot. Regardless of one's level of comprehension, the innate understanding is there, and the opposition merely verifies the understanding.

One of reasonably sound mind does not oppose what is not real—what does not exist. For this reason we see the Bible, the God therein, and His adherents opposed and attacked far more than tenets, beliefs, and scriptures of any other religion. Too, when other religions are opposed, political factors and social issues (ethnic strife, for example) are most often the primary catalysts; whereas Christianity is opposed in every part of the world based solely upon the tenets of the Bible.

Setting aside the sterile distinction of nominal Christianity, there are no Christian nations. There is no Christian army—no divisions, fleets, or wings. Christians hold but a small percentage of the world's finances and natural resources. Furthermore, no legitimate Christian group is mounting terrorist attacks of any kind, let alone those we now see so often designed to kill as many men, women, and children as possible. Yet Christians and the precepts of their Bible still are opposed the world over.

This is because the living God who has created all things and made everything appropriate in its time has also set eternity in the hearts of all people (Ecc 3:11), a fact that can be either comforting or chilling depending upon the response within the individual heart. Further, since the creation of the world His invisible attributes, His eternal power, and His divine nature have been clearly seen, being understood through what has been made, so that they are without excuse (Rom 1:20). Again, a truth that can be either comforting or disturbing depending upon the disposition of one's heart.

Jesus, speaking of His atoning death to come upon the cross, said, "I, if I am lifted up from the earth, will draw all men to Myself." He was lifted up on the cross, and now we see that, indeed, He has drawn all people unto Himself. This cannot be true, some argue, simply because the majority of the people in the world never have been followers of Christ from that day until now. This, though, reveals a failure to understand what is happening on both the spiritual and temporal plains.

Consider what happens when an overwhelming conquering army captures a city or state and then demands absolute submission to their own laws and rule. Some will submit in obedience and perhaps even join the new regime in some function or role. Others, detesting the new authority and resenting its presence yet fearing to try to fight it, will flee from it or otherwise try to stay as far from it as they can. A third group, however, will resent the foreign presence, refuse to submit, but then begin fighting against it with every weapon and tool at their disposal, whenever and wherever they can.

So we see three distinct groups, each taking very different courses of action and yet all for the same reason. All three groups are drawn to the invading force. This we can know simply because none would take whichever course of action chosen were it not for the presence and demands of the occupying force. While submission, flight, or fight represent three different responses, all result from being drawn by a singular force.

The same holds true with the gospel of Jesus Christ. All people are drawn to Christ just as He promised they would be. Some see the comfort, peace, the blessings of unconditional love, and the light of life eternal and embrace the Way of their Lord and take their place in His Kingdom. Others, being drawn but resenting what is demanded of them, flee or stay as far away from the new King and Kingdom as they can. A third group, though perhaps even more resentful and surely more militant, is drawn and comes forward, but they come forward to do battle. The King they cannot reach or harm, so they attack His Word, His symbols, and His followers with whatever weapons they have and by any means available. Attacks range from the low level persecutions such as mocking or harassment, the use of debate and media to try to turn as many as possible away from the Way and Word of Christ, the use of legislative power to curtail expressions and actions of faith, and then to the extremist opposition in the utilization of the martial power of state or militias to imprison and to kill. All is happening in our world even as I write. Yet the peace of God, which surpasses all comprehension and is given in abundance by Him to all who follow and walk in His Way, is never ruled by fear and is not subject to exterior circumstances.

Understanding the source of, and reason for, all opposition to our Lord, His Word, and His people should fortify the spirit of the true believer. For with understanding, the inner peace of God can only be enhanced and the blessed assurance of soul only deepened. The opposition is sustained and intensified only because the truth of the Word of God has remained unchanging, unerring, and the same yesterday, today, and to be so forever. Opposition will remain because the promises within the Word have never failed and continue to be honored and verified even today.

He who was called a Nazarene kept His promises to go to the cross for all people, to rise after three days in the grave, and then to draw all people unto Himself. All who truly know Him, who live in Him as He lives in them, will know that He delivers on His promise of peace, and that the peace He gives is not as the world gives and will not succumb to anxiety and fear (John 14:27). On this holy day of Epiphany, His peace and His salvation should be foremost in our remembrances and reflections. For as the angel said to the shepherds in the hills of Bethlehem, "Today in the city of David there has been born for you a Savior, who is Christ the Lord." Then the angel was joined by a heavenly host, which said, "on earth, peace among men with whom He is pleased." And Simeon, holding Jesus and looking into His eternal eyes, who said, "My eyes have seen Your salvation." Promises kept and prophecies fulfilled going back from that night six hundred years to the prophet Jeremiah, and seven hundred years to Isaiah, and a thousand years to David. Indeed, if we look and seek, the promises go back further still. For it was through Abraham that "all the nations of the earth will be blessed." This speaks of a blessing profound and timeless, touching those of every nation, tribe, and tongue. Such a blessing is only to be found in Him who demonstrated and proved through action, by compassion, and in blood-atoning sacrifice His genuine love for all people. This was the blessing of the Messiah, the one to be called "a Nazarene," who loved all people and taught us to look not upon the outside of people but into their hearts instead.

What, then, of the prophets and the Nazarene in verse 23? Just as with other verses of Scripture that have been singled out over the years by doubters and critics bent upon proving biblical error, herein lay no threat to the inerrancy and infallibility of the Bible. Indeed, the only dilemma comes in discerning which of several possible explanations is the most likely fit.

There are frequent references in the Bible to books or writings that have not survived but that we know existed and were passed around and read in ancient times. One obvious example is the Book of Jashar. Another is the apostle Paul's letter to the church in Laodicea, referred to in Colossians 4:16, which has not been found. The greatest likelihood would seem to be that Matthew was quoting one of the numerous, frequently-read prophetic books that was well known to his readers at the time but did not survive. Further, we know that not all the words of the prophets were written down. Prophets spoke more often than they wrote, and the oral tradition has been strong in the Near East, most of the rest of Asia, and in Africa from the earliest times. Stories, proverbs, and prophecies were more often passed down through the generations by word of mouth than by pen and parchment. Matthew may have been quoting a prophecy that was never written down but would have been well known to his first-century readers. Note that he wrote as if he expected them to know what he was referring to. As for the Jews of the time, we can be sure that they did know.

Another possibility is that Matthew, rather than referencing a particular text, was alluding to the "Branch Prophecies." The Hebrew letters NZR form the word "branch" and also are prominent in the words "Nazareth" and "Nazarene." The prophecies are found in Isaiah 4:2 and 11:1, and in Jeremiah 23:5 and 33:15. All speak of a "Branch" as a righteous descendant of David who would establish His justice and His rule and would bring salvation to Judah. Those espousing this view suggest that Matthew saw in Jesus' hometown a mark of His identity as Messiah, the righteous Branch from the house of David.

Skeptics, detractors, and scoffers will continue their efforts to persuade as many as possible of biblical fallibility. They are driven by a relentless spiritual catalyst. What should be remembered, regarding not only those verses most frequently targeted by them but the whole of Scripture as well, is that an understanding of ancient history, language, cultures, and context will invariably leave one with a clear answer or with numerous plausible explanations in matters otherwise unclear amid modern conceptions and presumptions.

Let us remember too, in our reflections upon this day of Epiphany, that the greatest and most revealing epiphany in the history of the world has been before us throughout these chapters. It is an epiphany offered to all people with partiality or preference given to none, and one revealing knowledge, understanding, and counsel on all matters. Not that it answers all questions, which it does not even claim to attempt. Yet for all questions and challenges that must be engaged in a life fully lived, the answers are to be found therein if one is willing to seek with his mind and heart fully opened. This epiphany for all people of every nation, tribe, and tongue is the sacred Word of God. In the Bible is to be found the Way of the living God passed down to us by the voices and hands of those faithful to Him through the centuries of unfolding revelation.

"Odd, the way the less the Bible is read the more it is translated," C.S. Lewis observed. Odd, too, we might add, that the most criticized and attacked book in the history of the world remains the best-selling book of all time. The Bible has been banned by governments and continually attacked by many of the most influential individuals, institutions, and entities the world over. Yet still it is printed and still it sells, and in far more translations, styles, and themes than were available in C. S. Lewis' day.

We should ask and contemplate how this is possible. For no book by any author has faced the formidability of the array of forces that have aligned against the Bible and not merely survived but thrived and increased against the multifarious onslaught to a degree commensurate with the attacks on Holy Scripture. The Bible survives, thrives, and continues to be translated into more languages even today solely because its source is not of men and its message is not of this world.

The epiphany of truth therein is the Way of Heaven, offering to all the knowledge of the Creator of all things who is without beginning or end and the counsel of the living God with whom there is no variation or shifting shadow. The power of the Word of God is irresistible, and His Kingdom stands unassailable. To all today who would attack His sacred Word or His followers, what follows is offered in the love and peace of our Lord Jesus Christ.

For the better part of two thousand years, the combined powers of the Satanic forces of wickedness in the heavenly places, some of the greatest among empires and nations, and the most powerful of people and institutions have been unable to destroy, or even to slow the spread of, the mere earthly manifestation of the Word of God, that is, the perishable material upon which His Word is written. Further, even when employing the most fearsome powers of state, this combined force has been unable to eliminate the adherents of the sacred Word. Whether utilizing force or varied forms of word, reason, and persuasion, the combined powers have failed even to stem the swelling tide of those who claim His Word and call Him "Lord."

Heed the words of the great swordsman, Miyamoto Musashi, "Think without any dishonesty, and think deeply." You, whether utilizing force or intellect, cannot even destroy the easily perishable earthly manifestation of the Word of God or the devotion of hundreds of millions of people to that Word. How, then, do you like your chances in going against Him who holds within Himself the Word and who is the Word? Against Him who gave the Word, sustained the Word and His people against all opposition, and who created all things and controls all forces of the universe? Do you truly desire to meet Him as an adversary? Life on earth is short, like a vapor that appears for a little while and then vanishes. Think deeply and think honestly.

The epiphany of Scripture is vast and multifaceted. The epiphany reached its culmination and emerged in its fullness, however, in the Advent of our Lord Jesus Christ, the beloved and only begotten Son of God. "For of His fullness we have all received, and grace upon grace." (John 1:16)

John continues: "For the Law was given through Moses; grace and truth were realized through Jesus Christ. No one has seen God at any time; the only begotten God who is in the bosom of the Father, He has explained Him." In the Torah, the Law, the prophets, the history, and in the poetry and wisdom books, God revealed much about Himself, His will, our world, and about the endeavors and true nature of Man. Yet only with the Advent of Jesus Christ, the Light that came down and shined in the darkness, was the true Way of God revealed and made known in full. For in Jesus we received not only the commands and counsel of God, but there saw the embodiment of the gentleness, compassion, loving-kindness, and forgiveness that is the essence of God and the true Way of Heaven. In the conjoining of those attributes, moreover, we see the quintessence of genuine love. For in Him was love defined and love exemplified. In His love extended freely to all regardless of ethnicity, status, gender, or age, and the giving of Himself to be lifted upon a cross and die as the atoning sacrifice for all people, we receive the "grace upon grace" poured out from Heaven in Him. In His resurrection we see the conquest of Man's most feared enemy, the earthly death awaiting all people. Therein, too, is revealed the truth of His promise and His power over all forces in the universe.

On this blessed Epiphany, reflect once more upon the fullness of the epiphany in Jesus Christ. Examine yourself and look forward to the year ahead. How far and for how long are you willing to follow the guiding light of whatever "star" He may set before you? What gifts will you prepare to lay before Him?

Paramount in the epiphany that is Christ Himself is the commitment and disposition with which we are to conduct ourselves in accordance with His example and command. Those anticipating in the Messiah a King to rule with the manner and vestments of earthly monarchs were to be baffled or even disappointed. For the eternal King of the everlasting Kingdom established Himself as the antithesis to such, saying, "The Son of Man did not come to be served but to serve, and to give His life a ransom for many." So let us go forward with the commitment and will to serve all people in His name. To lay down our lives for Him in this way is the greatest of the gifts we can set before Him and is one that resonates into eternity.